Front cover design by Julie Sato
Book design by Brad M. Bucklin.

Printed by BricHouse Publishing., in the United States of America.
ISBN: 979-8-9920771-9-3
First printing edition 2025.

BricHouse Publishing
265 East Orange Grove, Suite C
Burbank, CA 91502
bradmbucklin@live.com

This book is dedicated to my parents Joan and Harlan Rector, for their unending love and support. They always allowed me the freedom to make my own choices and pursue my dreams.

I love you both with all my heart.

Forward

"Hollywood is a town renowned for its narcissism, fakery and illusion. It is also a place where dreams can be realized. Through one's journey and pursuit of fame and fortune, one meets many types of people, the pretenders, the wannabes, people with talent and people without talent. There is of course, the genuine article - an individual with both talent and intelligence and an abundance of charm. Jeff Rector is such an individual. I first met Jeff many years ago and later we starred in a Lionsgate horror film together, The Darkening, aka The Black Gate. (Chapter #29).

Through the years, I've been privileged to watch Jeff's rise through the ranks of Hollywood; he has remained a working actor and award-winning writer, director and producer always pursuing and perfecting his craft. He has appeared in over a hundred and fifty films and television shows.

But while I celebrate his varied career achievements, it is the man himself that should be extolled above and beyond. Jeff has succeeded in doing all of this - and he now can add to his litany of crowning achievements with this book, which I am honored to be able to grace with this Forward. Jeff has retained his sense of modesty and humility through the halls of recognition and grace. I am proud to call him my friend. You are a man and an artist to be reckoned with, an inspiration to us all." - *George Saunders*

George Saunders is an accomplished actor, writer and producer with over thirty-five screenplays produced including The Hard Corps starring Jean Claude Van Damme for Sony Pictures. George is also very proud to have worked with the Navy Seals through the Coronado Special Warfare Center and can be seen in the Tom Clancy action/thriller, The Hunt for Red October."

I Was A Playboy Rabbit
and Other Stories
A
B-Movie Memoir

By: Jeff Rector

Table of Contents

Introduction

First, this book isn't one of those Hollywood tell-alls about what celebrities I've slept with and how much cocaine I used to do in the 80's.

Okay, maybe a little.

Truth is, I never liked cocaine. I'm already hyper-active and whenever I did it, it shot me through the roof. No thanks. I did smoke some pot and took a hit of acid with my girlfriend one time.

She was a dental hygienist and one day she talked me into taking the acid, smoking some pot, climbing into the dentists chair with her, doing some nitrous oxide (laughing gas) and having sex. I won't say my teeth got any whiter, but it was a pretty wild ride. Literally. Spit, rinse and repeat.

I've always been a very sensual individual, so there may be some portions of the book relating to certain relationships and encounters that happened along the way, but that's not what this book is about.

It all started when I was introduced to Playboy magazine as a young man. The colorful images of the beautiful and titillating Playmate Centerfolds, and of course, the award-winning articles. Just kidding. I never read the articles.

This book is about my journey through life and how I've managed to realize just about every vision and dream I've ever had for myself - and you can too. First, you have to start with a vision or dream of what you want out of life. What do you want to accomplish? And most importantly, what career path do you want to take in order to make a difference in the world. Whatever that is you have to want it with all your heart, be 1,000 percent committed to it, and above all be persistent! This is especially true in acting or the performing arts world because these types of jobs are the most difficult to be successful in. You just have to remember one thing. "You can do and be whatever you want in this world, don't let anyone tell you you can't!"

My favorite billboard has a picture of Abraham Lincoln on it. Above his head in large capitol letters are the words FAIL. FAIL. FAIL. Underneath Lincoln's picture is just one word. PERSISTENCE. Lincoln ran for Congress ten times and was rejected every single time before finally getting elected in 1860 to become one of our greatest Presidents ever. Can you imagine facing that kind of adversity for years, but believing in yourself enough to keep going to finally win the Presidential election? Persistence.

How did I do it? God only knows. Literally. God has played an important part in my life since I can remember. I was raised Christian Protestant (specifically Presbyterian). My father taught Sunday School and years later ran a church Youth Group. We went to church every Sunday and I joined a Youth Group when I was in my teens. It was a great group of kids. As I got older, I asked if I still had to go to church every Sunday and my father said you will until you're 18 and an adult when you will be making decisions for yourself. I remember when I turned 18 my father said c'mon Jeff we're going church. I said, I'm 18 now remember? I think I'm going to sleep in this morning. My father looked at me, frowned and took the rest of the family to church. I went back to sleep.

I got into a lot of trouble as a kid. Once, when I was thirteen, I was arrested for stealing a watermelon from the local market. I'm thankful for my loving and forgiving parents and a loving and forgiving God. I know what you're thinking, how can I write a book about petty larceny, sex, drugs and Hollywood and still be a good Christian? I said I was a Christian, I never said I was a Saint.

Let's be clear, I'm not some spiritual Guru that's going to anoint you with ten ways to instantly change your life. What I do hope, is to be able impart a few pearls of wisdom that I've learned along the way that may be helpful. I've been around long enough to at least know how life mostly works. At the writing of this book, I've reached the ancient milestone of 65-ish. I rarely admit this to anyone especially my agent. Thanks to some really good genes and managing to stay in relatively good shape, most people think I'm much younger, and I'm ecstatic about that. Unfortunately, by writing this book and admitting that to you now, I've just blown the facade and illusion of my youth to smithereens. Another lesson I've learned is that you're as young as you feel. In my head I'm still that eighteen year old kid excited about the future, what it may hold, and the adventures and experiences still waiting to happen.

One of my favorite sayings is "When one door closes, another one opens." I can't tell you how many times this has been true in my life. Meaning that everything that happens to us good or bad is for a reason. When something bad happens, we think that it's the end of the world. What looks like a bad accident or set of unfortunate circumstances that affect our lives in a negative way, ultimately sets in motion another series of events that will ultimately enrich our lives and sometimes, change them for the better. Another similar saying is, "Every dark cloud has a silver lining." No matter how dark and menacing the storm (your situation) seems to be, there will be a good reason for that storm and you just have to ride it out knowing that something good will come from it. No matter how dark it is in the tunnel, there is always a bright light at the other end.... unless you allow yourself get trapped in the tunnel.

Life is a rollercoaster ride with ups and downs, twists and turns, but we are all just along for the ride. It can be thrilling and exciting and sometimes downright terrifying. But it is out of our control beyond the conscious day-to-day decisions that we make as human beings.

This first part of this book takes place during a brief period of time in my life in the mid eighties when I moved to New York City to pursue my acting career. I had done relatively well as an actor and model in Los Angeles up to that point, but my work had leveled off and I didn't feel as though my career was moving forward. After moving to NYC, I worked a series of waiter jobs in order to support myself, eventually getting hired by Playboy Enterprises to be a Playboy Rabbit (the male version of a Playboy Bunny). I worked as a "Rabbit" for Playboy's New York *Empire Club* which would turn out to be the experience of a lifetime.

A lot happened during that period in NYC and this volume will share that and other crazy stories from that time. When the *Playboy Empire Club* eventually closed in 1986, I stayed in NY for two more years before moving back to Los Angeles to start a new chapter in my life where the story continues in the second part of the book.

Anyone who writes a book about themselves, (or any topic for that matter), hopes that at the very least, it will be well received. I hope this is the case. If just one person reads this book and has a better outlook on life, or has gleaned a little wisdom from my stories, or at the very least, got a chuckle or two, I'll feel that writing this book wasn't in vain.

Are you ready? Buckle up, this going to be an E-Ticket Ride. Please keep your arms and hands inside the ride at all times. Here we go...

Chapter 1

In the Beginning
My First Agent

I got my first agent a few years after graduating high school. My family had just moved to LA from Bloomfield Hills, Michigan, where I first attended a private high school called Pontiac Catholic. My parents sent me there even though our family was Christian/ Protestant. Having priests and nuns for teachers was weird since we weren't used to that in the previous public school system. But I adapted

quickly and ended up having a "hell of a good time." Forgive me, Father, for I have sinned. After my first year in private school, my

Taft High School Yearbook

father was offered a job in a big-time ad agency in Los Angeles. It also came with a considerable pay raise. So the Rector family packed everything up and moved to the San Fernando Valley. My sophomore year of high school was at William Howard Taft in Woodland Hills, CA. No nuns or priests there. I had a ball! I went from Catholic School Girls to *Fast Times at Ridgemont High*. Totally awesome!

After graduating High School, I became a Tour Guide at *Universal Studios*. It was the dream job that every actor or actress wanted. You're representing one of Hollywood's top motion picture studios with an easy and automatic path to being "discovered," signing a contract, and being a movie star, right? Wrong! Once hired, we quickly realized that the *Universal Studios Tour* and *Universal Pictures* that make the movies are very different organizations.

Universal's Classsic Monsters

Universal Pictures is known for all the classic monsters such as *Frankenstein and his Bride, The Wolfman, The Mummy, Dracula, the Creature from the Black Lagoon, The Invisible Man* and The *Phantom of the Opera*. The Universal Studios Tour was just that, a tour around the studio backlot. Don't get me wrong, being there was really fun and

Jeff on set as a Tour Guide at Universal Studios

exciting, but it turned out to be a minimum-wage job riding around outside in a tram on some sweltering summer days.

People working at *Disneyland*, playing characters like *Mickey Mouse* and *Donald Duck*, make the same money. At Universal we were nothing more than amusement park employees. I could write an entire book on my experiences as a Universal Tour Guide, but I will leave those stories for a prequel.

I stayed on the Universal Tour for a few years but got really burned out. There was nowhere to go from there but down. I told my father I still wanted to work in Hollywood; he had a few connections since he worked in the ad business. He talked to a friend of his, *Jack Yopp*, who was the President of a commercial production company named *Sandler Tape & Film (STF)*, which produced commercials. Jack agreed to let me work part-time for the company to see how it went. I wound up working there for several years. Jack was a great guy, and we became good friends. I loved it! I was now actually working in Hollywood! I worked at STF as a production assistant. I ran errands and sometimes worked the video equipment to record the auditions when they were casting. I was a Jack-of-all-trades, learning about every aspect of production.

Bruce Willis and ***Ed Beheler*** in ***The Last Boyscout***

One day, Jack called me into his office and said he needed me to run a special errand. I was to pick up an actor flying into the airport to shoot a commercial the next day. *Jimmy Carter* was the President of the United States at the time and an actor, *Ed Beheler*, from Texas, was a Jimmy Carter look and sound-a-like, making a lot of money impersonating the President. While excited about my task I was running late in picking him up due to heavier than usual traffic.

He was waiting at the airport curbside; everyone around him were staring because he looked just like the President. I opened the back door of the company car and he got in. I apologized for being late, and he said, "No problem, the flight was delayed getting in, and I haven't been waiting very long." Whew, dodged a bullet on that one! I had to drive him to his hotel to meet with the clients and was also running late for that. So I pushed the pedal to the metal to make up for the lost time. Thank goodness, the freeway traffic was light, and I was able to speed right along.

Suddenly, I heard a police siren and looked in my rear view mirror to see the Highway Patrol's flashing red and blue lights. Fuck! I pulled over. Shit, I'm screwed. I would be late now, and a speeding ticket could cost me my job. Double fuck!

I rolled down my window; the officer approached the car. He looked me in the eye and said, "You were driving twenty miles an hour over the speed limit!" Thinking quickly, I said, "Yes, officer, I know, I need to get the President to his hotel asap! The officer laughed and said, "Good one!" I point to the back seat, and the officer looks in and sees Jimmy Carter, the President of the United States. The actor smiled and waved at the officer, who was stunned. "Oh, of course! Sorry to have stopped you, sir!" And he immediately waved us on.

I hit the gas so hard I almost broke my foot. We sped away into the night before the officer had a chance to realize that he'd been had! Needless to say, I got "The President" to his meeting on time.

Another eventful day at the production office, I helped a well-known casting director with her casting session. She said I was handsome. "Have you ever thought about being an actor?" I said, "Oh yes, I did a lot of plays in High School!" She said, "Do you have an agent?" No, I said, "We just moved from Michigan, and I don't know anyone here." "Let me make a call and talk to a friend of mine who's an agent for commercials." I said, "Okay, great! Thank you!" She set me up with a meeting with an agent named *Evelyn Schultz*.

In our meeting she was lovely and polite. We talked for about twenty minutes and she finally said, "I'll be honest with you: other than school plays, you have no formal training as an actor. You're a good-looking kid, but there are a lot of good-looking guys your age with a lot more experience."

She was right, and then asked,"Are there any unique talents you have that might help us?" I said, "I do a lot of sports, and I'm an expert skier!" She said, "That's great, but that's not enough, sorry. It doesn't look like I can help you." Dejected, I said, "Thank you very much for meeting with me." I got up and turned to leave, then turned back to her and said, "I don't know if this means anything, but I'm an identical twin." She just about fell out of her chair, "What? You have a brother that looks just like you?" "Yeah, we're twins!" She said, "Now that's something I can work with!"

We signed a contract, and I had my first Hollywood agent! She started sending me out right away and I got a good response from casting directors. I started booking a lot of modeling jobs.

Jeff's early modeling photos

Now, you have to understand that I still had no formal training as an actor, just a few bit parts in a couple of High School productions. But now that I had a Hollywood agent that was all about to change.

Chapter 2

Agents and Managers

There are two types of artist representation in Hollywood; a Talent Agent, and a Talent Manager. Actually there's a third type they're called Bullshit Artists. These are people who represent themselves as a talent agent or manager to either bilk naive actors, dancers, singers, and musicians (take your pick) out of their money or, worse, to sexually prey on actors, dancers, singers, and musicians that will often do anything for the promise of a part or a gig. These charlatans are more prevalent than you might think and cast a long and sleazy shadow on the rest of the legitimate talent reps in the business.

Here is the difference between a Talent Agent and a Talent Manager. A legitimate talent agent has to be a signatory to the Screen Actor's Guild, the guild or union that all professional actors belong to that protects them from getting ripped off, abused, or taken advantage of. A talent agent receives ten percent (10%) of any work they get you. 90% of 100% is better than 100% of nothing. Most of the time (not always), the production company will pay an additional 10%-20% above the negotiated talent rate, which goes to the agent and doesn't come from the actor's salary or day rate.

The talent manager, however, will take 15-20% of the actor's fee whether they had anything to do with getting the job or booking in the first place. Let's say your talent agent gets you a commercial. If there isn't an additional agency fee that pays your agent, that agent's commission will come out of your pocket. If you also have a manager, you have to pay that manager out of your own pocket, even though your talent agent got you the job. You just paid an additional 15-20% to someone for doing absolutely nothing!

That's where most talent managers make their money, from actors getting work from an agent or the talent themselves if they got their own booking. Many lower-end managers take on as many clients as possible to have the chance to milk off as many actors as possible. Sound unscrupulous? Whoever said Hollywood was scrupulous? If you sign a contract with a manager, you'd better know what you're getting (or not getting) and be sure they're actually going to help you advance your career and get you some auditions. Any Agent or Manager who asks for any money upfront is a scam artist! Run away as fast as possible.

It's very difficult for newer actors to get good representation unless you are somewhat established and have good credits. After getting rejected and being told time and time again that you don't have enough experience, when a manager approaches you and says they'd love to represent you, the actors take the attitude, "Oh well, it's better than nothing." And it is. The problem is, if you aren't getting any work on your own, and are depending on a manager to get work for you, you're right back where you started in the first place since their main job is to manage/mentor you and help groom you for greater success. I've never had anyone groom me. I learned the right and wrong ways to do things independently and slowly built up my career. But early on, I too fell into the alluring trap of having a talent manager and quickly realized they're nothing more than a shiny, smiling, lying piece of dog shit. Too dramatic? I think not. Hollywood can be a cutthroat, dog-eat-dog business; it's not all rainbows and unicorns.

The good news is that it can be a very exciting and fulfilling career if you get the proper breaks. Also, even if you sign a contract with a talent agent or manager and realize they aren't meeting your expectations, you can quickly get out of it. You write them a letter saying that you hoped it would be a great working relationship, that it's not meeting your expectations, and that you would like to discontinue your professional relationship. Don't say, "You suck and I want out!" (even if it's true). It's always better to take the high road and be professional, even if the other party isn't. Not all agents and managers are created equal or are well-liked. Some of the meanest and nastiest agents and managers are sometimes the most effective in Hollywood, just like lawyers. But you didn't hear that from me.

Chapter 3

JAWS 2

One of my very first auditions from my new agent was to read for a top-secret project at *Universal Studios*. Little did I know that I was about to read for the sequel to the blockbuster, *Jaws*. I'm glad I didn't know ahead of time because I probably would have lost my shit.

I went over to Universal and read for the casting director. They liked me and brought me back in for a callback. Whether I

got the job or not was great because it proved to my agent (and myself) that the studio liked me and that I had some talent. I auditioned for the role of *Roy Scheider's* son in the movie. Scheider played *Sheriff Brody* in the original *Jaws*, the hero who eventually blows

Roy Scheider **as** *Sheriff Brody*

up the giant shark in the film.

Jaws 2 takes place five years after the original movie, and they needed an eighteen or older actor who could look young enough to be a 16-year-old. That was me since I looked young for my age.

Steven Spielberg did not direct the sequel, so the studio gave it to a highly respected writer and director named *John Lee Hancock*. I got the callback, which went great, but I didn't get the part. I was satisfied because I was so new to the business that I didn't think I would get it anyway. So they cast the film and started shooting in Martha's Vineyard on the East Coast. I forget all about it. A few months later, my agent calls me and says that Universal was looking at the dailies[1], and they didn't like what they were seeing.

They fired Hancock and hired a relatively new French director named *Jeannot Szwarc*. Jeannot later directed such masterpieces as *Somewhere In Time* with *Christopher Reeve*, *Jane Seymour*, and *Supergirl* with *Helen Slater*. Jeannot would also direct many hit TV shows like *Grey's Anatomy*, *Bones*, *Criminal Minds*, and *Designated Survivor* with *Keifer Sutherland*.

My agent called me and said that Universal wanted to see me again because they liked me the first time around. Once again, I'd be reading for the part of Sheriff Brody's son Mike. Woo Hoo! Thank you, Lord! I've been given another incredible opportunity to star in a *Jaws* movie for Universal Pictures. Always a realist, I also understood the odds of getting the part were slim as the

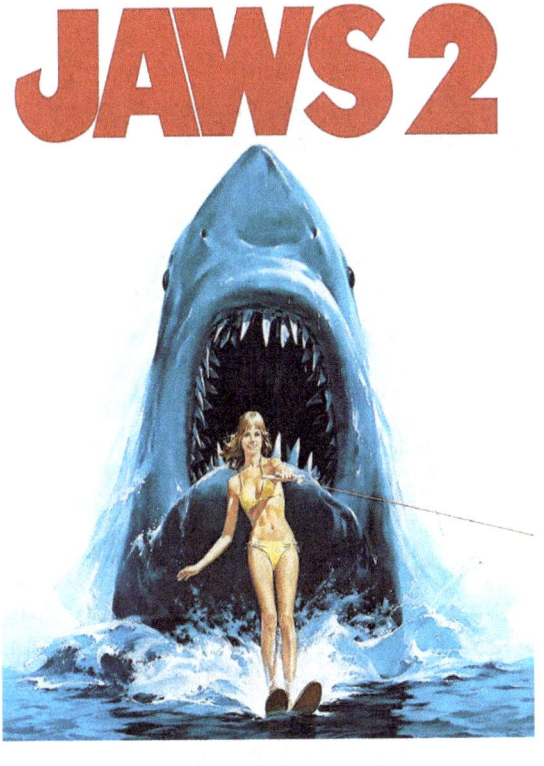

competition would still be stiff, with most other actors having way more experience than I did. So I went back to the studio. They had my name at the guard gate. I checked in, and I'm directed to one of the many production offices, a different location from where I

1 Dailies are bits and pieces of the movie that have already been shot and edited so the studio can see how the filming is going and how it looks.

originally auditioned.

Usually, when you go in for a reading, there are a bunch of other actors in the hallway waiting to audition as well. I recollect that there were no other actors there. I'm sitting there alone, and I'm nervous as hell. Usually, an actor is given a script or "sides" in advance to prepare for the audition. [2] Because this was still a top-secret project, no sides were provided in advance; it was a "Cold Reading," meaning you were given the sides in the office and asked to audition with little or no preparation. I'm trying to remain calm when the casting director, *Shari Rhodes*, came out and invited me into the casting office. I followed her in, and she introduced me to another woman named *Verna Fields*.

Verna was one of the top casting directors for Universal. She handed me two pages of a script and informed me this was different from the actual movie script since they were doing some rewrites. Verna said, "Look them over and let me know when you're ready." I said, "Okay," and looked at the sides. It was a pretty straightforward scene. A high school student is at a podium giving a heartfelt speech to his classmates. I read through it several times and told Verna I was ready. She said, "Are you sure? You can take more time if you need it." I said, "No, I'm ready." She asked, "Do you have any questions?" I said, "No, it seems pretty straightforward." She said, "Okay, anytime you're ready."

I wanted to jump right into the audition for several reasons: number one, I felt that I had a pretty good handle on the scene, and two, because I was so nervous my heart was about to jump out of my chest and I wanted to get it over with as quick as possible. So I was sitting in front of the two women and started reading the scene. I finished reading, and they both just stared at me for a moment. Then Verna said, "That was very good, Jeff. Would you mind reading again for a few more people?" I said, "Sure." So Verna and Shiela lead me down the hallway into another office. This time, four people were sitting in the room. Now I was reading for six people. Again, I was brand new to the business and very naive about the process. I had already given a good read, so I was much more relaxed now and

---

2"Sides" are a small portion of the script (usually three to five pages).

feeling really confident. I read it again and felt even better about my audition than I did the first time. I got a little choked up because it was a very emotional scene. There were two men and two women that hadn't seen me previously. One of the men said, "Excellent job, Jeff!" I said, "Thank you." I was feeling pleased and quite relieved.

Richard Zanuck and ***David Brown*** on the set of ***Jaws 2***

Shiela said, "Can you please wait outside for a minute?" I said, "Sure," and I went outside in the hallway.

I found out later that the two men were *David Brown* and *Richard Zanuck*, two of the top studio executives and Hollywood legends. *David Brown* was one of the original Producers of *Jaws* and produced other hit films like *The Player, Deep Impact*, and *Cocoon* alongside Richard. In addition, *Zanuck* produced *Driving Miss Daisy, Planet of the Apes, Dark Shadows, Clash of the Titans, The Verdict* and the *Eiger Sanction* with *Clint Eastwood*.

I was glad I didn't know who those guys were when I auditioned because I might have choked and blown it. After a few minutes, Shiela came out and said, "Well, everyone really likes you, and the producers want to fly you down to Florida to read for the director, *Jeannot Szwarc*. "What? Really?", "That's right. We'll be contacting your agent with all the details. Congratulations, Jeff, go get 'em!" I thanked her and walked out of the office building back to the parking structure. Woo Hoo! Fucking A! I am going to be starring in the new *Jaws* movie as *Roy Scheider's* son. When I got home, I called my agent, Evelyn, to tell her the good news. She congratulated me and said that she had already gotten a call from Universal and that production would contact me directly with all the flight information. I would be flying to Pensacola, Florida (the location had changed from Martha's Vineyard), and meeting with the director there. I was over the moon! I couldn't wait to tell everyone!

As promised production called and told me to meet the new cast and crew on the *Universal Studios* backlot, (my home turf), where we'll be shuttled to the airport.

I got to the meeting area, and about fifteen people were waiting for the shuttle. Some young actors my age and some older people that were crew members. I looked around, and I'm stunned to see a very recognizable face. *Christopher Knight* was world famous for playing the iconic role of *Peter Brady* on the hit TV show *The Brady Bunch*. He was talking with another young actor, and I introduced myself. "Hi, I'm Jeff Rector. I'll be playing Sheriff Brody's son; what part are you guys playing?" They both started laughing. I think that's rude, so I asked, "What's so funny?" They looked at me and said, "We're all reading for Sheriff Brody's son. What? Didn't Shiela tell you you were reading for the director?" I said, "Yes, but she didn't tell me other people were reading for it!" They laughed again and said, "Welcome to Hollywood, Jeff!"

At that point, I laughed too. "Yeah, I thought it was too good to be true." The shuttle bus arrived, and we all climbed aboard; at least I'd made some new friends.

On the bus ride to the airport, I started to process all this new information and realized that Christopher Knight was just too well-known from the Brady Bunch to be believable as Roy Scheider's son. So it was really down to me and the other actor, Mark Gruner. Suddenly, my chances of actually getting the part were now 50/50. I'd take those odds any day. Better than Vegas. At least I knew who my competition was. Imagine if I had gotten down to Florida not knowing that other actors were still in consideration. All in all, no matter what happened, it would be a fantastic adventure. I was pretty damn excited.

We arrived in Pensacola and checked into the Marriott Hotel. It was a beautiful resort right on the beach. We were greeted by one of the production people who checked us in and gave us our room assignments along with a white envelope with some cash in it. I asked what the cash was for, and she said that's your per diem. "Per diem, what's that?" I ask. "That's the daily amount of money you get to pay for food when you're working on location. "Oh, of course!" I pretended to know what that was, but she wasn't sold. "You have the rest of the day off, so just relax. You'll be meeting with the director tomorrow since they're shooting today. Good luck!" "Thank you so much!" I headed up to my room, put down my luggage, and decided to do some exploring.

There was a large bar and restaurant in the Hotel. I walked into the bar and recognized several production people from the bus ride. I looked around and saw my two new friends, Christopher and Mark. They saw me and waved me over. They were both drinking a beer. I said, "Hey guys! How'd you get beers?" They said, "The drinking age in Florida is 18. You're 18, aren't you?" I said, "Hell's yeah!" I ordered a beer and made a toast, "To playing Sheriff Brody's son." Everyone, "To playing Sheriff Brody's son!" We toasted and laughed.

I was introduced to other cast members, some of whom I recognized from movies and popular TV shows. One actor named *Gary Dubin* was incredibly nice, and we would remain good friends for many years. In *Jaws 2*, it was primarily teenagers on summer vacation in Martha's Vineyard because they had already shot some footage that would still be used in this newer version even though they were now shooting in Florida. I also learned that Sheriff Brody's son Mike had a girlfriend in the movie; she was a really cute actress named *Donna Wilkes*, who had done a lot of work. We were all at least 18, playing 16-year-olds. Because of the child labor laws, if you're under 18, you can only work a certain amount of hours, and the studio has to provide on-set teachers for a child actor's education. If you're over 18, you're considered an adult, so studios don't have all the shooting restrictions and don't have to pay for teachers, private schooling, shorter work time, etc.

Donna introduced herself and said I should come by her room later to get better acquainted since we might be working together.

Later that day I knocked on her door. She answered it wearing a very sexy silk bathrobe. I was unsure if she was wearing anything underneath, but I didn't ask. I came in, and she said, "So we may be working together." I said," That's right, that'd be cool!" She said that *Mark Gruner* (my competition) had already come by her room with some coke—the drug, not the soft drink. I said, "Oh," and thought, was she expecting me to bring some party favors of my own? I had tried marijuana by then, but certainly not cocaine. I said, "Oh, cool," not knowing how to respond. Was I suddenly being indoctrinated into the ways of Hollywood? I wasn't quite sure what was supposed to happen at this meeting so I was quite nervous.

She then went over to the desk in the room and grabbed a circular container with some pills in it. She pulled out a pill and popped it in her mouth. I had never seen a pill box that looked like that before. I said, "What are those?" She said, "Oh, these are my birth control pills." I said, "Oh. Cool!"

Idiot! Is that the only thing you can think of to say? "Oh, cool? As I said, I was nervous; this was all new to me.

We chatted for a while, had a few laughs, and then I left. I felt like an idiot. Was she waiting for me to make a move or kiss her? If she had kissed me, I definitely would have gone for it; as I said, she was really cute and might be my "make-believe movie girlfriend." Also, part of me wondered if this was some test to see what I'd do. Remember, this was a major motion picture for Universal Studios. Part of me said, be professional here, Jeff; you don't want to do anything to fuck this up.

The next day, I was sitting in my room, when the phone rang. It was one of the production crew; she said that Jeannot (the director) was finally ready to meet me. So I went down to his room. He was very friendly, and we briefly chatted. He asked questions to get to know me. I didn't mention that I was in Donna's room yesterday. Jeannot gave me some new sides; this time, they were from the film already in production. I took a few minutes and then read with the director. He gave me some notes and direction and I read it again. It didn't go as well as the first audition with *David Brown* and *Daryl Zanuck*. It seemed as though he wasn't getting the performance he was looking for. He said, "Thank you, Jeff," and that was it. I went back to my room.

Christopher Knight and I were notified later that we did not get the part and that it went to Mark Gruner. Fuck! I had already told all my friends, family, and anyone who was listening that I'd be playing Roy Scheiders, son. Double Fuck! Well, at least the anxiety had subsided, and the decision had finally been made. I knew what room Christopher was in and decided to knock on his door. He answered and let me into his room. He said, "Well, I guess you got the good news too?" I said, "Yeah, fucking Mark!" We both laughed. Misery loves company.

The difference between Chris and I was that he was already a major TV star from *The Brady Bunch* and already had a ton of money; I was just getting started in the business and was broke. We're watching TV in his room when a re-run of *The Brady Bunch* comes on. We had a big laugh over that one. Universal flew us home the next day, and that was it. Game over. But I did get a three-day, all-expense paid trip to Florida from the studio that produced *Jaws*. I had impressed two top studio executives enough to send me to Florida and got a small taste of what being a movie star feels like and I wanted more.

I learned two life-changing lessons. Number one, I was a good enough actor to get that far. Number two, I knew now that stardom was attainable, and I was just getting started. I was even more excited for the future and what lay ahead.

I have crossed paths with Christopher many times over the years. I also found out years later that *Susan Olson*, who plays *Cindy Brady*, was in my High School graduating class, and *Maureen McCormick* (Marsha Brady) had a best friend I briefly dated in High school, and we would all hang out together. Today, I play tennis with *Lloyd Schwartz*, the son of *Sherwood Schwartz*, who created *The Brady Bunch* and *Gilligan's Island*. Who knew? Hollywood is a small town, and I'm always surprised who knows who or is six degrees of separation from *Kevin Bacon*.

I ran into Donna many years later at an autograph show where there was a *Jaws 2* reunion. We had a couple of laughs together, talking about my ill-fated trip to Florida, although I didn't bring up being in her hotel room or her birth control pills. My friend Gary Dubin, who I stayed friends with for decades, tragically died of cancer in 2016. I also found out many years later that Mark Gruner, the kid who actually got the part of Mike, had such a horrible experience working on the film that he gave up acting altogether. Are you kidding me? This dream role would have made me an instant overnight movie star. Oh, well. Things happen for a reason, as they say. "Welcome to Hollywood, Jeff!"

Top: **Shark Attack** - Below: *Gary Dubin* **and Bruce the Shark**

Chapter 4

Double Trouble

Okay, let's recap. I had just gotten my first commercial agent because I mentioned to Evelyn Schultz that I had a twin brother, and she signed me as a client. Depending on the markets and usage, I started booking some commercials that would be very lucrative and stayed with Evelyn for about a year. I did some more commercials and a lot of modeling. Things were going pretty well. I was curious why Evelyn wasn't getting my twin brother Jerry and I any twin auditions, but I didn't think much of it.

A short time later, I met with another talent agent who handled commercials, television, and motion pictures. I thought it was time for a change since Evelyn only got me a few TV or movie auditions (even after Jaws 2). She asked me who I was currently with, and I told her Evelyn Schultz represented me. She said, "Oh, I know Evelyn, she's very good!" I said, "Yes, she is, but I'm more interested in TV and movies." She said, "I can help you with that!" I said, Great! Oh, and the other thing is that she never got me or my twin brother any twin auditions." There was a moment of awkward silence. She said, "You have an identical twin brother?" I said, "Yes."

She then informed me that Evelyn had identical twin sons about our age. She had signed me as a client to keep Jerry and I out of the Twins market as long as possible. That's why she got so excited when I told her I had a twin brother.

I signed with a new agent, and she started getting us a lot of Twins auditions. At the very first Twin audition we attended, we met her twin sons, Keith and Kevin. I was really mad at them at first, but then I realized she probably never even told them what she had done. Evelyn was right to be afraid of us as we were much better looking than her redheaded twins. Every time we saw them at an audition, I'd say, "Be sure and tell your mom, the Rector brothers said hello!" Imagine sabotaging our careers to protect her sons. I guess you could at least say that she was a good mother!

The very first commercial together (that we stole from the Schultz boys) was for *Oldsmobile*. I know what you're thinking, "What's an Oldsmobile?" *Oldsmobile* was a brand of automobile manufactured by *General Motors* (GM) along with *Chevrolet, Cadillac*, and many other top American brands. Founded in 1897 as the *Olds Motor Company*, it was one of the longest-lasting brands for 107 years and was eventually phased out by 2004. At the time we did the commercial, Oldsmobiles were popular as ever.

The advertising agency cast Jerry and I, a faux mother and father, and another actor to play our best friend named *William "Billy" Smith Jr.* who was the son of actor *William Smith Sr.*, a well-known television and film actor, who starred in *Any Which Way You Can* with *Clint Eastwood* and *Jeffrey Lewis* and *Red Dawn* with *Patrick Swayze* and *Charlie Sheen*. I would work with William Sr. many years later in the action film, *Never Look Back*. I would also

Jeff and Jerry Rector in a McDonald's commercial

work with *Jeffrey Lewis* on *Double Impact* and *Charlie Sheen* on *Wall Street*.

In the commercial our parents were sitting in the front seat, and the three of us were sitting in the back. Our TV father pulls into a gas station, and the attendant comes over and says, "Fill her up?" (I still don't know why they refer to a car as a "her" and not a "him.")

The commercial was shot back in the day when there was no such thing as self-service. Gas Station "attendants" would fill your car with gas, check the oil and other fluids (if requested), and even clean your windshield. Virtually unheard of today unless you're approached on a street corner by a homeless person with a squeegee.

You would sit in the car until the attendant filled up the gas tank, then you'd pay the attendant, and off you went. Easy, peasy. Pretty luxurious, right? So, in the commercial, the attendant says, "Fill her up?" And our Dad says, "Sure!" The attendant then looks in the back seat and sees the three of us sitting there and says, "Enough room back there for you mooses?" We all reply in unison, "Sure is!". That was it. We got paid about $600.00 for the day for smiling and uttering the words, "Sure is!" What was more important was that by doing that commercial, the three of us qualified to get our Screen Actors Guild card.[3]

Back then, it was not unheard of to make $15,000, $30,000,

---

3 The Screen Actors Guild is the union for actors that would guarantee a certain daily acting fee and residuals or royalties paid to actors if commercial, motion-picture or television shows play nationally or around the world.

or even $60,000 a year (per commercial) depending on how many times the commercial ran, how many cities (markets) it played in, and for how long. It was possible to make a six-figure salary if you booked four or five good national commercials in one year, although I never did. Every thirteen weeks, a new "holding fee" had to be paid to the actors if the producers wanted to continue running the spot on the air. They could also pay a holding fee to the actor and decide later if they wanted to run it. The third option was "dropping" the spot or canceling it if the producers chose not to run it anymore. I think they ran that particular commercial for at least two years, which meant some serious coin at about $24,000 a year. Not bad for three 16-year-old kids who just smiled and said, "Sure is!"

At the time, I was the only actor in the family, and Jerry was a musician and drummer. As twins, however, we were a valuable commodity in Hollywood whenever they needed identical twins. We were both good athletes, in great shape thanks to our parents' great genes. As the commercial continued to run, we got residual checks or a holding fee every thirteen weeks. One day, my twin brother Jerry came to me and said, "Hey, this acting thing is pretty good! I think I'll be an actor too!" I went, "Uh no, that's what I do. I'm the actor in the family! You're a great drummer; stick with that!" This would become a great bone of contention for me for many years. Although the twin's schtick was very lucrative for us, the twins' jobs were few and far between. So, if Jerry was an actor as well, we literally had to compete against each other for "single" jobs. I used to joke, "That's all I need is another actor in Hollywood that looks like me!"

Against my better judgment, my parents said that it would only be fair to share my agent with my brother since we were making money together. I became pretty resentful of having to share my agent; after all, I was the one who worked hard to get them in the first place. I felt as though he was riding on my coattails, and in actuality, he was.

Here's how it worked. Because we had the same agent (mine), we decided to split up the auditions. I'd go on one; he'd go on the next one. The problem with that scenario was that my audition could be for a small company, paying little, and the next one that Jerry was up for could have been worth tens of thousands of dollars. It wasn't fair or balanced. Also, it meant I was getting 50% fewer auditions by sharing them with my doppelganger. My agent didn't care because either way, they'd get their commission on the job, no matter which one of us booked it. The upside was we were actually getting more work as twins than I was getting on my own because there was so much competition.

When we auditioned together, we had a nickname for ourselves. As an introduction we'd say, "I'm Jeff Rector and I'm Jerry Rector and we're the Rector Set!" Referring to a popular toy at the time called, wait for it, an *Erector Set*. So when we said that we were *the Rector Set*, it always got a chuckle from the casting director, producers, and advertising people. It was a cute gimmick that made us stand out from the other twin actors, which possibly led to more bookings.

Once, we did a really funny spot for Eggo's frozen waffles. At the time, the slogan for Eggo's was, "Hey, leggo of my Eggo!" We played a scientist who cloned himself to keep all the frozen

Spec Commercial for Miller Beer

waffles for himself. But the experiment backfired because he created so many clones of himself that they all wanted the Eggo waffles. At the end of the spot, there wound up being about eight different clones of us as scientists yelled, "Hey, Leggo of my Eggo!"

We even did a political spot for Propositions #215 & #216,

which was an initiative to cut property taxes for Californian residents. I represented Prop #215, and Jerry represented Prop # 216 in a mock political debate. We argued back and forth about the merits of each of our propositions, as the discussion got more heated. At the end of the spot, the political moderator interrupts us and says, "It seems like both of your Propositions are pretty much the same and will raise property taxes, costing Californians millions!" We looked at each other and then at the camera, embarrassed like we got caught with our hands in the cookie jar.

The spot was hilarious and ran like crazy right up until the election. Both Propositions #215 & #216 were ultimately defeated by the public vote, and we were pleased to know that we helped save Californians millions in increased property taxes. I found it interesting that a simple, comical commercial could help sway public opinion that much. Jerry and I would continue to work together doing the twin schtick. Why not? I was willing to ride that gravy train for as long as possible.

Chapter 5

New York City - The Asphalt Jungle

I was getting restless living in Los Angeles having been working in Hollywood for over 6 years as an actor and model, and yet my name wasn't exactly a household word.

I had just graduated from Moorpark College with an Associate of Arts Degree in Drama and Telecommunications. I was an award-winning state and national speech champion but didn't want to continue with my education, so I felt like it was time for a change. The year was 1983.

My parents (Harlan and Joan) moved my sisters (Dana and Amy) from California to Riverside Connecticut as my father would now be working in Manhattan. I figured it was a good time to give

New York a shot. Since my parents were already on the East Coast, it seemed like an easy segue to the "Big Apple." My father was one of the top voice-over guys in NYC at the time. Voice-over (or narration) is the voice over the action in a commercial, TV show or film, basically, the voice that sells the product or service. Voice-overs are also the "Tagline" at the end of a commercial. For example, in the Prego Spaghetti Sauce commercials, for ten years my father said the tagline, "Prego, it's in there!" Because of talent residuals or royalties, he got paid every time they played the commercial and he made a lot of money just off of that one job. Ka-ching!

A voice-over artist could easily make six-figures in salary and residuals if he/she got a few good national television commercials. My father was also chosen as the original "signature voice" of the History Channel (THC) for the first four years of its inception. He'd record the audio commercials, promos and introductions to THC's lineup of shows. This was extremely lucrative and suddenly he

The Rector Family (L-R) Dana, Jeff, Joan, Harlan, Amy, Jerry, and Doug

was making more money with his voice than the 25 years working himself to death in the advertising world as an art director.

One of my favorite television shows was an AMC Emmy-winning drama called *Mad Men*, which was written, directed, produced and created by *Matthew Weiner*. Mad Men depicted what went on behind-the-scenes in the New York advertising world in the 1950s. This included drinking (alcohol), smoking cigarettes and having sex in the agency offices. Most of the big Agencies at the time were located on Madison Avenue, and so the Ad Agency guys were known as Mad Men. My father was an art director in advertising and was an Ad Man, except his agency was in Los Angeles and he didn't smoke, drink or have sex in the office.

Harlan Rector

After suffering a heart attack at age 44 from the extreme stress prevalent in the world of advertising, my father quit the agency and stumbled into the world of voice-overs by accident. Sometimes, as an Art Director, he would use his voice temporarily for the commercial copy when presenting an idea or concept for an advertising campaign to a client. He turned out to be a natural at it. Little did he know that this would lead to a new career and a whole new chapter in his life for both he and his family.

When he left the agency, he put together a voice-over reel and sent it to some of the Talent Agencies he had worked with over the years. One in particular was *The Don Buchwald Agency* (DBA). It was also one of the biggest and most prestigious in the city. They agreed to take my father on as a client if he moved to the East Coast. So he agreed. He moved my mother and my two sisters Dana and Amy with him. My twin brother Jerry, my younger brother Doug and I decided that the LA lifestyle was just too good to give up, so we gracefully declined and stayed in California.

My father quickly rose to the top of the agencies client list. When I finally decided to make a change and move to New York, he got me an interview with DBA. At the time, Don Buchwald was *Howard Stern's* personal agent and manager. I remember joking around with Howard at the DBA Christmas Party in 1984. I had no idea who he was; he was just this really tall guy with long curly black hair who looked like a rock star, but was hysterically funny. He was cracking me up with his stories about the days when he was trying to break into radio. Little did I know, that Howard would soon write these stories in a book called *Private Parts* that would become a best-seller, a hit motion picture and that Howard would become "The King of all Media," and one of the most successful radio/tv personalities of all time.

On my first trip to the City with my father, he warned me that walking on the street during the day and especially at night; some parts of the city could be very dangerous. His advice was to walk fast with a purpose and don't stop to talk or engage with anyone if you didn't know them. I laughed, "Okay Dad," I figured he was just being overprotective.

I would soon discover he was right, along with all the other harsh realities of living in the city of New York in the 80s.

My father and I were taking the subway to the agency where he was going to introduce me around and interview with the DBA agents for representation. Even though my father was one of their top voice-over guys I wasn't guaranteed to be accepted. I still had to sell myself.

We were on the subway platform and the train arrived. It had been raining that morning and everyone was wearing raincoats and carrying umbrellas. As the subway doors opened, two women slightly bumped each other's shoulders as one was exiting the subway and the other woman was entering. One woman turned back to the other one and said, "Watch where you're going Bitch!" The other turned and said, "What did you just say?", "I said, watch where you're going Bitch!" All of a sudden, they attacked each other and one woman knocked the other one to the ground and started stabbing her with her unopened umbrella. Now, these weren't two street urchins, they were well-dressed businesswomen.

I made a move to try and break them up, but my Dad

quickly ushered me inside the subway car before the doors closed. The subway train jerked forward and moved out of the station. As I looked out the window, the women were still fighting and no one seemed to notice or care. I turned to my Father.

Me: What just happened?
Father: I told you, you have to be careful when you're in the city. People get crazy sometimes.

I had never seen anything like it before. Two seemingly educated women, viciously fighting over a simple shoulder bump on a subway platform. That was my first but wouldn't be my last such experience.

Times Square 1980s

Most of the time when I was in the city, I walked the streets to and from an audition or for a job, as most people did. Everything is so close you don't need a car. But on the street, there is a real disconnect with people in the city that I have never experienced anywhere else. People were actually in fear of being mugged or assaulted or being taken advantage of in some way. Until it had happened to me and my brother I would have said you were crazy and that the city streets were safe. They were not.

At the time, I lived in Hell's Kitchen (not the cooking show) but a part of the city that was more dangerous than SoHo, Midtown or Uptown. It was also less expensive. I had to take whatever waiter jobs I could, in order to pay my bills until my acting career gained momentum. After all, I was starting from scratch in a new city, with a new agent and I had to make all new connections and friends. One of my favorite Nightclub's was called *Nirvana* and it was about six blocks away from where I lived, an easy walk home after a night of partying.

The great part about not having to drive in New York City is, you never have to worry about drinking and driving or getting a DUI. You can take a subway (not too late at night), a cab, or simply walk. Nirvana was my local Nightclub and I had many booze-fueled dance party nights with the local ladies. Oh, did I mention that NY Clubs are open all night? Stumbling out of a club or bar at 5:00 am or 6:00 am in the morning was commonplace.

One particular night, I left early around 1:30 am since I had to work the next day. I stopped off at my favorite Gyro fast food place (I don't remember the name) to get a delicious late night snack for my six-block walk home. Thank God I didn't drink too much that night.

I'm walking down 6th Avenue to 39th street (where I lived). I would turn right on 39th Street for about two and a half blocks to my walk-up. The apartments in NYC are called walk-ups because very few apartment buildings have elevators, so you have to literally walk-up as many flights of stairs to get to whatever floor you lived on. You didn't want to live on the 7th or 8th floor believe me. If you got downstairs and remembered you forgot something, you had to walk back up and down all those flights of stairs all over again.

As I walked home enjoying my Gyro I suddenly got this feeling (my spidey-sense) like I was being followed. I looked behind me and saw a group of four guys on the sidewalk, walking behind me. Not taking any chances, I spotted a payphone just up ahead. I stopped and took the phone off the hook pretending to make a call. The guys passed me and kept walking. A few of them stopped at the corner of 39th street and the other two guys crossed to the other side of the street. Whew! I felt a huge sigh of relief. It was just my overactive imagination (and the alcohol in my system) getting the better of me. I hung up the phone and made my way down to 39th street, turned right and headed down towards my apartment.

All of a sudden, my spidey-sense went off again and was overcome with this feeling of dread. I quickly looked back over my shoulder and saw that the four guys on either corner of 39th street were starting to converge on me. Remember, it was 1:30 am in one of the worst parts of town and there was no one else anywhere in sight. I looked down the very long block ahead of me, it was completely dark with no lights even on in the buildings. Looking back at them, I noticed there was a space between the two groups as they were on either side of the street coming towards me. In a split second, I decided to make a dash toward freedom right at them as they were converging on me since it was closer to 6th Avenue and I would have a better chance of being seen when they jumped me, rather than down a long dark street with no street lamps.

The two guys on the left were startled (the element of surprise) because the last thing they expected was for me to run right at them. As I got closer, they realized my plan and tried to close off the gap between me and them. When I got close enough to them, I hurled the rest of my Gyro in one of the guys faces which caused him to react and slow down as I sped up. I was just about between them, when one of the guys on my left, stuck his foot out trying to trip me. I jumped over his outstretched leg and ran. They turned around and started chasing me. I don't know how many blocks I ran, but they eventually gave up the pursuit. I'm quite sure that if I had been caught, (I only had eight dollars in my wallet), they probably would have beat the shit of me just because I didn't have enough money and I made them chase me to get it. I don't think I was ever that scared before in my life.

I was the first of five children in the Rector household, but I wouldn't be for long, because five minutes after I was born, my identical twin brother Jerry popped out.

He too moved to New York a few years after I did. I remember one very cold Winter's day and everyone was wearing heavy jackets and long overcoats. Jerry was on his way to a friend's walking down one of the fairly busy side streets that run through the city. In New York City it's not uncommon for people to just hang out on the street or in front of businesses, alleyways or on stairwells. In addition to the actual alleyways, there are smaller, dark hallways leading into certain buildings.

Jerry was walking down the street and passed a guy who quickly shoved him into one of these hallways, right off the street. There was another guy waiting inside. He pulled a knife on my brother and said "Where's your wallet?" Jerry said, "In my coat pocket." Without missing a beat, he slashed Jerry's coat pocket and his wallet fell out. Just then, some passerby saw what' was going on and yelled at the guys. "Hey! What are you doing?" As the guys were startled, Jerry made a b-line towards the good Samaritan and safety. Unfortunately, the thugs still wound up with his wallet. And this was in broad daylight about 11:00 am in the morning. You just gotta love New York!

Chapter 6

Subway Hero

Another day, as I pounded the Manhattan pavement auditioning for my next job. I got off the crowded subway and headed up the stairs to the street. I saw a mugger grab an Old Man. The mugger threw him face down onto the subway stairs. Of course, fifty people just walked by like there was not a cloud in the sky. Would they get involved? No friggin' way. I first started to yell at the guy.

"Hey! Get off him!"

So I grabbed him from behind and tried to pull him off, but the mugger had his arms wrapped around the Old Man still trying to get at his wallet. He was not budging, so I started to yell,

"Police! Police! Help!"

Finally, the mugger got scared and took off up the stairs. I helped the Old Man up.

Me: Are you okay?

Old Man: (Nothing, he's scared and shaking like a leaf).

I walked him up the stairs and low and behold, there are two NYPD cops with the mugger in custody. (They just happened to be at the top of the subway stairs, what are the odds?) I took him over to the cops.

Me: That's the guy officer, he tried to mug this old man in the stairwell.

Cops: (To Old Man) Is this the guy that mugged you sir?

The mugger gave the Old Man a threatening look.

Old Man: (Still scared shitless) No Time! No Time!

Cops: Sir, I need you to identify this man as the mugger.

Old Man: No time! No time!

Cops: Sir, if you don't identify this man and file a complaint, we can't arrest him and we'll have to let him go.

Old Man: No Time! No Time. (He began to sound like a broken record).

Me: Don't you understand sir, you have to file a complaint or they'll let him and go and he'll mug somebody else. Is that what you want?

Old Man: No Time, No Time. (Was that the only English he knew?)

Cops: All right, we'll walk him up the block and have a little talk with him, but we're going to have to release him. Sorry.

Sorry? They actually caught this guy and now they're going to let him go? I just risked my neck for this guy, and they're going to let him go?

Me: Can't I file a complaint? I saw the whole thing!

Cops: Sorry sir, the victim has to do it.

I looked at the Old Man and he just looked at the ground.

The cops lead the mugger away. The Old Man looked at me for a second and then ran in the other direction. I'm left standing there at the top of the subway stairs without so much as a thank you from this guy. I was like, what the hell just happened? It was just another day in New York.

If that wasn't enough here is another New York street story. I was walking to an audition in the morning in the middle of rush hour and I saw this homeless guy standing on the street corner. He undid his belt and pulled his pants down around his ankles. He squatted and started to defecate on the sidewalk like he was in the middle of the woods. Did I mention this was right in the middle of rush hour about 9:00 am on a major street corner? Did anybody stop and notice? Of course not. Everyone in New York walks around with blinders on. I of course stopped. How could I not? It was too surreal not to. I blinked and rubbed my eyes, but he was still there shitting on the sidewalk. I thought I had seen it all! Apparently not. After about a minute, another guy on the street stopped and said to the homeless guy.

Guy on the street: Man, ain't you got no respect for yourself?
Homeless Guy: (Nothing, just a grunt as he continues to crap on the sidewalk).

At that point, I'd seen enough. I shook my head and continued on my way. Also, I didn't see any toilet paper nearby and I wasn't going to wait and see what was going to happen next.

Now I knew why they call the city, the asphalt jungle. It was pretty wild and interesting living in New York in the '80s. But it was going to be a lot more interesting very soon.

Chapter 7

Tavern-on-the-Green

To support my acting and modeling career I worked several waiter jobs in between gigs. I had worked at *The Omni Hotel* for a while, as well as at *Nicole*, the French Restaurant and Brasserie next door. I went from there, to working at the world-famous restaurant *Tavern-on-the-Green, TOTG or The Tavern* (the Green being the grass in Central Park which borders the back patio of the restaurant). You could literally walk from the restaurant right into Central Park and vice-versa. It was kind of cool because in the summer when we worked the back patio, we could watch people playing Frisbee, running round with their dogs or women sunbathing in the park.

An acting buddy of mine from Moorpark College, *Curtis Nowitzky*, told me they were hiring waiters at The Tavern. Curtis and I were previously in plays together at Moorpark College and both wound up in NY at the same time. Tavern-On-The-Green is not only a major tourist attraction but one of the top restaurants in the city, doing huge business all year round. TOTG only hired new waiting staff, once or twice a year, and because it is such a huge banquet facility (27,000 square feet), they literally hire 80-100 waiters, waitresses, busboys and kitchen staff all at one time.

The Tavern was opulently designed with beautiful woodwork and decorated with old-world antiques. Hanging over the main Crystal Room, (an all-glass dining area) was a century-old chandelier made of green glass, said to have been owned by an Indian maharajah. In 1973, *Warner LeRoy* (son of the famous *Wizard of Oz* producer *Mervyn LeRoy*), took over the lease and traveled the globe to find these whimsical and ornate decorations to adorn the restaurant. It was like dining in a historic monument.

In its heyday, The Tavern-On-The-Green served more than 700,000 meals, bringing in more than $38 million dollars annually.

Warner died in 2001, he left the business to his wife, *Kay LeRoy*, and daughter *Jennifer LeRoy*. When the families operating license expired, the city sought competing bids. The LeRoys lost to *Dean Poll*, who operated the stylish *Loeb Boathouse Restaurant* overlooking the *Central Park Lake*.

It all came to end in 2009 when the legendary landmark restaurant found itself in bankruptcy court. Its $8 million dollar debt was recovered at an estate auction selling off the Baccarat and Waterford chandeliers, Tiffany stained glass, a mural depicting Central Park and other over-the-top décor that had bewitched visitors for decades. Since then, the restaurant was purchased again and is back in operation, which is only fitting since The Tavern-On-The-Green is one New York Cities most famous Historical Landmarks.

Curtis and I showed up at the The Tavern interview along with a hundred other wannabe actors, singers, dancers, etc. We were all waiting to interview for a job, so we could work nights and weekends and have our days free to audition and pursue our dreams in the entertainment industry.

There's an old joke, a guy and a girl are on a first date and he asks her where she works, and she say's "I work in a Coffee Shop", then she asks the guy, "So where do you work?" The Guy says, "Oh, I'm an actor!" The girl gets really excited and says "Really? Which restaurant do you work at?"

We're all there waiting to be interviewed. They handed everyone an extensive 5-page application form, which took over an hour to fill out. What is your experience? What restaurants have you worked for? What kind of cuisine have you served? It was incredibly in-depth and thorough. Fortunately, I had already worked at the *Omni Hotel* and *Nicole* the French Brasserie, so I was trained in European as well as continental service. I filled out the application and waited for my turn to be interviewed. There were several managers interviewing people, and were taking people in four at a time. An hour and a half later, they finally called me into the main dining room and I sat down with one of the managers.

I was excited, I couldn't wait to explain what an excellent server I was, and relish in the fact I was extensively trained. The manager looked at my resume for about 10 seconds.

TOTG Manager: "Okay pick up that tray and walk across the room."
Me: "Excuse me?" I said incredulously.
TOTG Manager: "Pick up that tray and walk across the room!"

The tray he referred to was a standard restaurant-serving tray that could hold about four large plates of food, but because The Tavern used metal covers over the food to keep the dinners warm, they were able to stack three times as many dinners on a tray. So instead of four dinners, which was the norm, we were expected to carry 12 dinners, which was also three times as heavy.

I was used to carrying heavy trays and because I was in great shape, I was able to carry the trays with only one hand.

Tavern On The Green's Famous Crystal Dining Room

So I picked up the tray with the 12 dinner plates and covers and I waltzed across the room and back and set it on the tray stand. I walked back over to the manager's table and sat down.

Manager: "Okay, you start training on Saturday. Next!"

And that was it. I was out the door. No interview, no social interaction, no looking at my resume to see my experience, just pick up the tray and carry it across the room. They didn't want a server; they wanted a workhorse to carry heavy trays of food from the kitchen to the dining room for eight hours (or more) at a time. I was insulted. All those years of training to be a great waiter, an hour to fill out their comprehensive application, waiting an hour and a half to be interviewed, and at the end of the day, all they needed was some muscle wearing an apron and a bow tie.

It was like training for years to be an actor and then asked to be in the background. No acting necessary. Just walk from here to there and keep your mouth shut.

So I'm standing outside the restaurant still reeling from what just happened. My friend Curtis who had just finished his interview came up to me.

Curtis: "So, did you get hired?"

Me: (unenthusiastically) "Yeah", but that was such Bullshit!"

Curtis:" Who cares, we got the job!"

Me: (snapping out of it) "Oh yeah, we got the job! WOO HOO!"

That next week we started training. Because of my of ballsy attitude and sarcastic sense of humor, I have always been able to make friends rather quickly. Most of the new hires as I suspected, were performers trying to pay their bills while following their dreams just like me, so we all automatically had something in common. I was single at the time and there were a lot of very attractive female servers, so that was a plus. They trained us on their particular style of service, read us the rules, the do's and don't s and made it quite clear that they could fire and replace any of us at a moments notice. One of the big ones was they were hiring us to be waiters, NOT performers and anytime our professional life got in the way of our work, we would be terminated instantly as there was a long list of other applicants waiting in the wings. It was a food factory, plain and simple. They knew we weren't there for a future in the food service industry and they made it very clear that we were all expendable.

Following the dining room training was the kitchen training and how we were supposed to order and pick up the food. All of us were jammed into the kitchen to be schooled by the Head Chef (I don't remember his name). Do this, don't do that, if you do this you're going to piss me off and you might not get your food right away, etc. He then went on to explain about the food expediter (this was the guy that took your dinner order and then actually set up the food on your tray to be carried out to the dining room). It was a very important job because the expediter kept the food moving and made sure it got out of the kitchen as fast as possible.

Once again, we're talking about a food factory that would serve thousands of meals on a weekend alone. The main expeditor's name was Jack, so the Chef kept referencing him saying pay attention to Jack. Work with Jack and he'll work with you. Any questions? Everyone was so intimidated at that point nobody dared ask a question and be put under the spotlight. Always the smart ass, I raised my hand.

Head Chef: Yes?
Me: You said that Jack is the main expediter right?
Head Chef: (sternly) Yes, so what's your question?
Me: Well, if Jack's the main expediter, what happens when Jack's off?
Head Chef: Well, in that case...

As he started to answer, there was a smattering of snickering and giggles, which quickly turned into laughter from all the waiters.

The Head Chef looked me straight in the eye; so I kept a deadpan expression on my face so that he wasn't sure if I was being a smart-ass or if I was asking a legitimate question. I could tell by his look, however, that he was going to be keeping an eye on me from that moment on. But it was worth it. When they let us go from the kitchen for a break, I got a lot of pats on the back, "Good one Jeff!" "That was hilarious!" etc. In that one act of defiance, I instantly made a lot of friends and everyone (for better or worse) knew who I was.

I had only been at The Tavern for about two weeks, but things were going great! I made a lot of new friends and was making more money than I had at any of the other restaurants and they fed us really well. At the time, MTV was in its heyday and was the most-watched cable channel in the world. Word got around that they would be producing the very first MTV Video Music Awards in New York City at the world-famous Radio City Music Hall. This was the most anticipated Award Show next to the Oscars and we found out that the after-party was going to be held at TOTG. The restaurant was abuzz with excitement. Everyone from *Michael Jackson* to *Bon Jovi*, to *Huey Lewis and The News* was going to be there.

The First MTV Awards

The Tavern management called for a staff meeting to inform everyone what the protocol was and what would be expected of us. This was a BIG DEAL, MTV and their sponsors would be spending hundreds of thousands of dollars on food and drinks for the A-List celebrities and their entourage to party after the Awards Show.

Everyone was excited to be able to serve and rub elbows with the musical elite, plus, because an automatic tip was added to the bill for large parties, the tips that night were going to be amazing. I was preparing my pitch for any TV or film directors and producers that would be there.

Then the A-Bomb was dropped, the schedule of the waiting staff was announced and I wasn't on it. Was this retribution from the Head Chef for my insolence during the kitchen training or was it just bad luck of the draw? Those of us that weren't scheduled for the event were devastated. Not only weren't we going to be at THE EVENT of the year, but we would also miss out on all the extra tip money for that night.

As I wallowed in self-pity, it suddenly occurred to me. If I'm not working that night, what's to stop me from crashing the party? The idea was of course completely insane. If I got caught, I would be fired immediately. Not only that, the security for an event like this, with that many celebrities, would be off the chart. But the more I thought about it, the more excited I was. If the security was too tight and I couldn't weasel my way in? No harm, no foul. I would just head back home knowing I at least tried.

By the time of the big event, I had gone over all the details in my head dozens of times. I knew that the party was starting at 10:00 pm after the awards show. I figured it would take about 30 minutes for everyone to Limo it over from Radio City Music Hall, so I figured, I shouldn't show up before 11:00 pm.

I also knew it was going to be an extremely classy event, so I pulled out my tuxedo (which I had for upscale catering jobs.) I was also modeling at the time and with the tux on, I looked like I just stepped out of a GQ fashion magazine.

Okay, next step, liquid courage. I took a couple of shots of tequila to calm my nerves and put me on track. I jumped in a taxicab and headed uptown to the main event. I got out of the cab and looked at my watch, 11:00 pm on the dot.

My adrenaline was pumping, I felt (and looked) like James Bond on his first mission. As I cased the surroundings, it was as I had imagined, a fleet of limousines dropping off celebrities and black-suited security guards at every orifice. I had inside intel though, because I worked there, I knew where all the kitchen and other entrances were. As I made my way around back of the restaurant I realized they were way ahead of me, there were security guards at every entrance and every back door. Shit! Now what? A lonely cab ride back to my apartment with my tail between my legs. At this point, the tequila started kicking in. I was a man on a mission. I kept working my way around the back. Remember, this was a huge restaurant with a lot of entrances. I came around to the outside patio (which as I mentioned, bordered Central Park).

It had rained earlier that evening and the patio was still wet. A few people were outside on the patio smoking cigarettes and I could see another black-suited security guard just inside the door guarding the patio entrance. They say it's all timing. I waited until the security guard turned his head to look back inside and I made my move. I jumped the short patio fence but slipped on some water and fell down. Half of my right leg got wet; I quickly got up and brushed as much water off my tuxedo pant leg as I could. A couple was standing right there in front of me and saw the whole thing. They looked right at me like, 'did you just jump the fence and crash the party?' I just shrugged and walked past them to the door, just as the security guard turned his attention back to the patio and looked me right in the face. I waved and smiled and without hesitation walked right past him. Luckily, the couple on the patio who witnessed my daring act kept their mouths shut.

I was in! Oh my God! I was in! I don't know if it was the

tequila or the fact that I infiltrated the biggest event in New York City that night, but at that moment, I felt invincible. I went straight to the Men's Room to catch my breath, regroup and dry my pant leg the best I could. I combed my hair, straightened my tie and I was ready for action!

I came out of the bathroom and went straight to the bar. One of my buddy's was bartending, he looked at me in my tuxedo.

Bartender: "Dude, what are you doing here?"
Me: "Shut up and make a margarita!"

Incredulously he made me the margarita and handed it to me. I nonchalantly replied.

Me: "I was invited by my agent. What did you think, I'd be stupid enough to crash this?"
Bartender: "Dude, you are so lucky!"
Me: "You have no idea!"

I winked at him and tipped him a dollar and I'm off to the races. Next stop, the buffet table. The event was even more opulent than I imagined. Prime rib, seafood, everything we had on the menu and then some. After gorging myself on the buffet, I went back to my buddy for another drink. I figured the fewer staff that knew I was there the better.

Bartender: "How's the party?"
Me: "What do you think? I'll give you all the details tomorrow."

He made me another margarita and I tipped him another dollar. When you're at a party like that, everyone assumes that you're somebody. I had an amazing time and met some really cool people. The party was raging until about 1:30 when I heard that there was going to be an after-after-party at the *Hard Rock Café*. Shortly after that everybody started leaving to go to the Hard Rock. At that point I thought, okay that was enough fun for one evening, I got away with it, it was time to head home.

Outside, I started talking with one of the Limo drivers who asked how the party was. I told him how cool it was and some of the people I'd met.

Limo Driver: "Are you going over the Hard Rock Party?"
Me: "No, I think I'm going to head home."
Limo: "If you want, I'll give you a ride over there, my ride here just canceled and I need to go over there anyway to pick someone else up."
Me: (without missing a beat) "Okay."

I got in the Limo and he took me over to the Hard Rock Café. By that point I had a pretty good buzz going and I was soaring with the eagles. We pulled up in front of The Hard Rock and the place was a madhouse. Paparazzi were on the sidewalk taking pictures of everyone getting out of the limousines, screaming fans were asking for autographs and this was 2:00 am in the morning on a Thursday. As you can imagine, there was beau coup security. Hard Rock Security opened my car door and I was ushered right up to the red carpet to the front door. The Hard Rock doorman acknowledged me.

Doorman: "Name?"
Me: "Jeff Rector"
Doorman: "You're not on the list!"
Me: "But I just got out of a limo."
Doorman: "Yeah, I saw, but you're not on the list".
Me: "But I just came from the Tavern-On-The-Green Party."
Doorman: "I don't care if you came from Mars, you're still not on the list! Can you step aside please?"

Just as I stepped back, *David Lee Roth* from *Van Halen* entered with several others. Even more celebrities arrived and went in. I realized that the gravy train was over and I wasn't as slick as I thought I was. I was just about to turn to leave when the doorman got called inside and another door guy took his place. I waited a few minutes until he let some people in and looked down at the guest list, I moved in right behind the group and quickly moved into the club with them as though I were part of their entourage.

I was in! Oh my God! I was in! I was two for two. Inside the Hard Rock was even more of a scene than the previous party. By this time everyone was pretty drunk or stoned (almost everyone in the entertainment business in the '80s was either doing cocaine or smoking marijuana or both). I entered the club looking for any familiar faces. I went upstairs to the 2nd floor where more of the rocker types had gathered. There was a smoky haze covering the

room and I could smell the aroma of pot mixed with cigarette smoke. Remember, back in the day, you could smoke cigarettes wherever you wanted to?

I went to the back of the room and saw David Lee Roth sitting next to *Huey Lewis* at a round table that seated about ten people. I sat down in one of the empty seats right across from them. Again, if you were at the party, everyone automatically assumed that you were invited and that you were somebody. I sat there for about half an hour just listening to these iconic rock legends of the day talking shit. I was mesmerized; it didn't get any better than that. Or could it? I had brought with me a little mini-bong that fit in my tuxedo jacket pocket and some choice green buds. I pulled it out, held it up and called out to Huey.

Me: "Hey Huey, want a hit?"
Huey: (Looking over at the bong) "Yeah man, I could go for that!"

I loaded it up, went over and sat next to Huey and handed him the bong. He took a hit and passed it to David.

David Lee Roth: Cool! (He finished the hit and passed the bong back to me) "Thanks dude!
Me: "My names Jeff, nice to meet you guys!"
Huey Lewis: I'm Huey and this is Dave."
Me: (With a laugh) "I know, I love your music!"
Huey & Dave: Thanks.

We hung out for another fifteen minutes when someone made the announcement that the party was over. Everyone started filing out and getting back into their limos to go home. I was just behind Huey as he got into his limo and I stepped forward just as he closed the door.

Me: Hey Huey, can you give me a ride home?
Security Guard: (Who pushed me back from the Limo) "Hey man! Step away from the car!"
Me: "But I was just hanging out with Huey!"
Security Guard: "Sure you were. Now step away from the car!"

Just then Huey's Limo pulled away from the curb and I shouted out after him. The security guard gave me a look like, yeah, you're a real close friend of his. Oh well, I was two for three. I poured myself into a cab and went home. The next morning, I woke up with a screaming hangover, but the night before, was one of the best nights of my life! I couldn't wait to get to work and share my adventure with all my jealous co-workers.

I admit the next day was pretty rough. I had the lunch shift and I had to be in early to set-up. Word got around pretty quick about me being at the party. If I hadn't reached all-star status with my peers by now, that definitely put me over the top. I was the envy of everyone. As I was setting up the dining room for lunch, one of the managers came over and asked me to join him in his office. Uh oh, what's this about? Now, as I mentioned earlier, there were several managers at TOTG, and some were nicer than others. Some

I had a really good rapport with, and some I did not. This was one of the shittier managers that I had a bad rapport with; I referred to him as my NEMESIS. We went into his office and sat down.

Manager: "So Jeff, do like working here at TOTG?"
Me: "Yes sir, I like it very much."
Manager: "You're fairly new here, aren't you?"
Me: "Yes sir, about two weeks. May I ask what this in regards to?"
Manager: "Well, it's my understanding that you were here at the MTV party last night?"

(Uh oh, here it comes!)

Me: "Who told you that?"
Manager: "Several of the staff and one of the managers who saw you here."
Me: (Trapped like a rat). Yes, as a matter of fact, I was here, (nervous laugh) it was quite some party!
Manager: "That's what I understand. I wasn't working last night."
Me: "You would have enjoyed it."
Manager: (really annoyed) "Tell me Jeff, how is it that a Tavern-On-The-Green waiter that's only been here for a few weeks, gets into one of the biggest, most private events in the city?"
Me: Well sir, my agent also handles Howard Stern and some of the biggest Soap Opera Stars in town. He thought it would be a great opportunity to meet some industry people.
Manager: (He cuts me off) Let me make myself perfectly clear Jeff. If I ever see you at any event while you're working here, you will be fired. We have a policy that prevents any employee from fraternizing at an event whether they have the day off or not. Am I making myself perfectly clear?"
Me: "Yes sir, I had no idea. It won't happen again."
Manager: Good. Now get back to work!"
Me: "Yes, sir, thank you, sir!"

Whew! I dodged a bullet on that one. I made it through the

rest of the day, went home and passed out.

As I mentioned earlier, there were a lot very attractive women working in the restaurant. One we'll call Suzie. (I have changed the names of several people out of respect.) Suzie was one of the Maitre D's, a step up from a waiter in both salary and prestige. The Maitre D' was the person who actually took the dinner order from the table and interacted with the guests. TOTG had a delicious Caesar Salad that was hand-made right at the table with the Maitre D' making the dressing right in front of the guests. I had seen Suzie a few times from a distance since we had not yet actually worked together. She was a few years older than me, a beautiful brunette with grace and class and also had a gorgeous body.

One day, out of the blue, I was assigned to her as one of her waiters. We worked well together and although I tried to get her attention, she was all business and took her job very seriously. It wasn't until several weeks later that I saw her taking a quick cigarette break. I told her I enjoyed working with her and would she like to go out for a drink sometime. She said she was seeing someone and that wasn't possible. Of course, she was, why wouldn't someone like her have a boyfriend. I felt like an idiot.

Several weeks went by and I ran into her again. She asked if I still wanted to have a drink. I said I thought she had a boyfriend and she said it didn't work out. She agreed to have a drink with me but made it very clear that she didn't want a relationship and that if anyone at the restaurant found out we were seeing each other, that would be the end of it and probably my job too. I said that was fine, I was good at keeping secrets.

We hit it off instantly and started dating regularly. I was really happy and wanted something more, but she kept making it clear that's not what she wanted. As long as everyone was happy, that was good enough for me, at least for the time being. Yet there was something peculiar about her that I couldn't figure out.

Whenever we'd go out, she would excuse herself and go to the women's bathroom, sometimes two or three times. I finally realized that she was sneaking off to do some coke. That's not what bothered me. What bothered me was her hiding it from me and that she wasn't honest about it. When I finally confronted her and asked why she felt she had to hide it from me, she said it was "her thing" and that it had nothing to do with me. But it did, because we were together. I really cared about her and I would have done a little toot here and there, no big deal.

As time went on, she said that she was feeling pressured by everything (not me) but everything else in her life. She was trying to make it as an actress too and said that I was working more (as an actor) than she was, and that made her feel weird. I said that didn't matter. If we were together, it shouldn't matter who is working more than the other.

Things started to get even weirder; even when it was obvious she was doing her little coke sessions she still tried hiding it from me. For me the real problem with her doing coke was that sometimes it numbed her body, usually affecting her sex drive. Several nights we'd come home after a wonderful dinner or night out on the town and she wouldn't be "into it" because of the coke. At that point, I said I love you, but you're destroying what we have. Are the drugs more important than I am? She said that she needed it to be able to maintain, and I said, "Then I have to walk away." I really loved her and thought that we would be able to work everything out, but that was it. Suzie wound up leaving TOTG sometime after that and I never saw or heard from her ever again. Unfortunately, this would not be the last problem I had with women who have substance abuse issues.

I stayed at TOTG for a while after that. Why not? It was a good job, with good money and I had made a lot of friends there. I had done several commercials, print jobs, and voice-over gigs and was really starting to gain traction as a working actor. The more I worked as an actor, the less I wanted to work as a waiter.

One night I was out late celebrating a new commercial job with some friends and had a little too much to drink. I stayed out longer than I wanted since I had to work early the next day. The alarm went off and I could barely move. Since I had never done it before, and I was working a lot of double shifts to get ahead financially, I decided to call in sick. The good thing about TOTG is, there was always an abundance of waiters to cover shifts and I owed it to myself to take the day off. Remember my "NEMESIS"? The manager that called me on the carpet for the MTV party? Out of all the managers working that day, he answered the phone.

Manager: "Hello, Tavern On-The-Green?"
Me: "Hi, it's Jeff Rector..."
Manager: "Good morning Jeff, how can I help you?"
Me: "I really don't feel very well and I'm not going to be able to come in this morning."
Manager: Oh, I see...well, unfortunately, Jeff, we've had a number of waiters already call in sick today and we're really short-staffed."
Me: I know, but I've never called in sick before, and I'm really not feeling very well..."
Manager: That decision is yours Jeff, but if you don't come into today, don't bother coming in ever again. Do you understand?"
Jeff: "Yes."
Manager: "So what would you like to do?"
Jeff: "I guess I'm coming in."
Manager: "Good call. You can do your morning shift and then go home."
Jeff: "Okay."
Manager: "See you soon."

BASTARD! Shit! My head felt like an atomic bomb had gone off in my brain. Suck it up Jeff! So I took some aspirin, had some toast and I dragged myself into work. I barely made it through my shift. All I could think about was getting home and going back to sleep. I was just finishing my last table when one of the other managers (one of the nice ones,) his name was Mike, came over to me.

Mike: Hey Jeff, I'm sorry to have to do this to you, but we got stiffed on the afternoon shift and we need you to do a double.
Me: "What? I called in sick this morning and was

threatened to be fired if I didn't come in, with the understanding that I would only work the morning shift."

Mike: "I know. We have no choice, normally it wouldn't be a problem, but we have double the number of normal reservations today. I know it sucks."

Me: I don't know if I can make it Mike, I'm exhausted."

Mike: "I would never ask you Jeff if I had any other option."

Me: "You've always been very good to me Mike, I'll do the best I can."

Mike: "I appreciate it Jeff. I'll make it up to you."

Help! Somebody, anybody, Help! At this point, I am beyond exhausted. It was a beautiful spring day; Central Park was full of people and I was working the back patio where we had more reservations than usual without enough staff to work it. I started to set up the outdoor patio for the early dinner rush and kept looking out at Central Park. Several people were flying kites, some guys were throwing around a football, people were laying on blankets having picnics, it was the perfect idyllic day and I was stuck with a massive hangover working a double-shift. I was setting down the silverware and napkins, but my attention kept going to the peacefulness of the park, I couldn't stay focused. My body was trying to work, but my brain was saying, 'go find a nice shady spot and just go lay down in the park and close your eyes.'

One of the other waiters came over to me and said, "Jeff what are doing? Keep working, the managers are watching you."

I looked over and saw Mike and my "NEMESIS" staring at me. I looked down at the table, I looked over to Central Park, which was beckoning me. I looked back over to the managers, back to Central Park, I felt like I was in a daze. Without realizing it, I took my bow-tie off and walked towards the managers. I went right up to my "NEMESIS" and handed him my bow tie.

My Nemesis: "What's this?"
Me: "I'm done."
My Nemesis: "What do you mean you're done?"

Me: "I'm leaving."

My Nemesis: "What do you mean you're leaving, for the day?"

Me: "No, I'm leaving for good, I'm done. Good luck!" (my NEMESIS frowned, turned and walked back inside).

Me: (To Mike) "You've always been good to me Mike and I appreciate it. Take care."

I shook his hand.

Mike: "Good for you. Good for you Jeff, you take care as well."

And with that, I walked off the patio into the park and found a nice shady tree where I laid down and went to sleep. It was several

Tavern On The Green's back patio bordering Central Park

years before I went back to *Tavern-On-The-Green* with some friends to have dinner. That time, I was the one being waited on.

Breaking into the business in "The Big Apple" was tough. Even though I was with one of the best agencies in town, it took me a year and a half of pounding the pavement before I was able to book my first national commercial for RCA Records. I remember, I was at some production office for another audition and I hadn't heard from my agent about RCA. I was in the restroom in one of the stalls thinking that if I didn't get the commercial, I would return to LA with my tail between my legs.

At the time, I had started dating an actress from one of my

acting classes. She was very pretty, full of life and had beautiful curly blonde hair. She was a Buddhist and introduced me to the rituals of meditation and chanting. I was raised as a Christian in the Presbyterian faith and didn't really know that much about Buddhism. But I really liked this girl and I have always prided myself on being able to keep an open mind.

Then the oddest thing happened, there I was sitting in the bathroom stall with my pants around my ankles and I started chanting, Nam-Myoho-Renge-Kyo, Nam-Myoho-Renge-Kyo, Nam-Myoho-Renge-Kyo. All of a sudden, my pager went off, (pagers were the newest technology at the time and would beep if someone was trying to reach you). I looked down at the number, it was my agent. I jumped up and ran into the production office, (after pulling up my pants) and asked to use their phone. My agent told me I had booked a national commercial for RCA. "Thanks" I said calmly and hung up the phone. WOO HOO! After a year and a half of constant auditioning, it was about time! Although I was going to be getting "residuals" I still had to keep a regular job.

I had been living in Manhattan for close to two years. The difference between L.A. and New York was that everything's a lot more expensive in NYC, especially the housing. I couldn't afford my own place so I shared one with a guy and his Parrot in Hell's Kitchen. Hell's Kitchen was not a very nice part of town, (as I previously mentioned), but it was all I could afford at the time. My roommate was a chef at the restaurant where I was working at night as a waiter and he was a *Grateful Dead* fanatic! He loved the Grateful Dead so much that he collected every song and every album ever manufactured. Good for him. Unfortunately, that meant that all he ever listened to was The Grateful Dead. Over and over and over ad nauseam. To this day, if I hear a Grateful Dead song, I will fly into a fit of uncontrollable rage and kill anyone in a six-foot radius. So there I was, running around Manhattan auditioning, doing extra work once in a while and playing waiter at night. But that was all about to change.

The difference between extras in Los Angeles and the extras in New York are, a lot of the L.A. extras are "Professional." That's what they do for a living. They have no interest in being a movie or TV star, or even just being an actor. It's an easy paycheck for sitting around the set all-day or walking back and forth in the background of a scene. The extras in New York are real, classically trained actors just trying to survive in pursuit of their dreams. There was a different level of respect for extras and actors in N.Y. This was where I went from being a simple extra to getting stand-in jobs.

A stand-in is an extra that is the same height, weight, look, complexion and hair color as the star. A stand-in literally stands-in for the star while the production team sets the lights, sound and camera angles or camera movement for a particular scene. It also allows the actor to have time to relax and go over their lines for the upcoming scene. This is very tedious work and goes on all day long until all the scenes for that day are shot and the day is finished, (wrapped). When the star starts shooting for the day, the stand-in is right there. When the star is wrapped, so is the stand-in. If the star has a day off, so does the stand-in and usually with pay.

My first experience was when I was asked to stand-in for a day player on the *Nora Ephron* film *Heartburn*. I had never heard of the actor I was standing-in for, but I was happy for another days work at a higher pay rate. The actor had a "little scene" where he came into the apartment and robbed everybody at gunpoint. After the scene was over and the director yelled cut! I remember thinking, hey, this guy's pretty good. The guy, the one I had never heard of, was *Kevin Spacey*.

Little did I know that one day as *Kevin Spacey's* stand-in would lead to not only a series of stand-in work on some of Hollywood's biggest films but also lead to some principal speaking roles as well.

Chapter 8

Wall Street

One day out-of-the-blue not long after my first stand-in job a casting director called me saying they were casting for *Oliver Stone's* next film after his hit Vietnam War drama *Platoon* that starred *Charlie Sheen*, *Tom Berenger*, and *Willem Dafoe*.

She said this Oliver Stone film was about insider trading on the Stock Exchange and was going to be called *Wall Street*. She also said they were looking for an actor to be Charlie Sheen's stand-in and was I interested? Was I? Although I was a few years older than Charlie, we were about the same height, same look and build and both had the same short, dark brown hair.

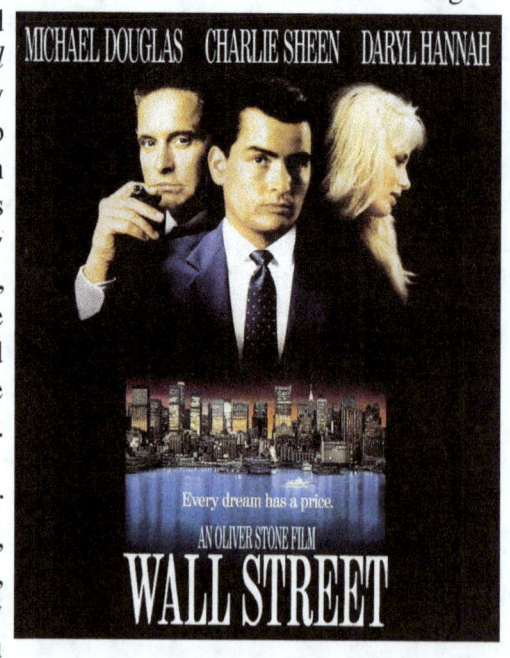

The casting director was very specific. "Jeff, you are perfect for this, but Oliver Stone is very particular. They want you to stand-in for Charlie Sheen tomorrow, the first day of shooting. But if Oliver or Charlie don't like you for some reason, that's it, you're gone." "I understand," I said, "I'll be on my best behavior," I added with a laugh. She didn't laugh. You can imagine everything that was going through my head that night. I didn't sleep much. The big day arrived. I showed up on the set and was introduced to Oliver and Charlie. We went right to work. The first days filming consisted of a lot of exterior shots of Charlie going to work, getting on the Subway, walking on the street, etc. I did a lot of running around.

One of the first rules of stand-in work was not to talk to the "star." They were focused on more important things than shooting the shit with their stand-in. Never speak until spoken to. If they want to talk to you, they will. Your job wasn't to be the Stars "best friend"; it was to stand under the hot lights for hours on end so the Star didn't have to. Needless to say, I didn't say boo to Charlie. I was right there next to the camera on every scene waiting to be called in. Traditionally, stand-ins are referred to as the "Second Team" and the stars are of course the "First Team." When they call for the "Second Team," you'd better be right there. If they have to call for you a second time you're in trouble. A third time and you will be replaced.

The first day we shot for about 10 hours, at the end of the day, the 1st A.D. (Assistant Director) *Steve Lim* came up to me and said, "Good job today, we'll see you tomorrow, your call time is 7:00 am."

Woo Hoo! That was it, I was in! Working on *Wall Street* was an amazing opportunity and great experience. Not only did I get to work with Charlie Sheen and Oliver Stone, but the film boasted an all-star cast with *Michael Douglas*, *Martin Sheen* (Charlie's father), *Daryl Hannah*, *Terence Stamp*, *James Spader*, *James Karen* and *Sean Young* to name a few. These were all incredible actors I had grown up watching and admiring, and here I was working with them as part of the production team. It was an actor's dream come true.

I enjoyed cracking up Michael Douglas every day with my non-stop collection of dirty jokes. I was part of the crew, a family put together to make Hollywood magic. Since every movie was different, with a different cast and crew, you would never have the same experience twice. Wall Street was, and still is, one of the most memorable and enjoyable films I have ever had the pleasure of working on. During the three months of working on the film Charlie eventually started to open up and we became friends. Since we literally were working downtown on Wall Street, it was a long and expensive cab ride. The only other choice was getting jammed and squashed like a sardine on the subway during the morning and evening rush hours. Charlie frequently gave me a ride home after work in his own limousine.

One night I talked Charlie into going to one of my favorite clubs in Manhattan in the middle of Times Square. Remember the place I was walking home from when I almost got mugged? That

was the club, Nirvana. It was decorated like a Middle Eastern palace with tapestries on the walls and cushions and pillows all around the club to sit on. It also had a gigantic glass window where you could look out over the city lights of *Times Square*. Me, Charlie and a friend of his, Donnie, who was also working on the film got to the club around 10:00 pm and right off the bat we started doing tequila shots. After a few minutes, I saw a cute brunette girl and went up to her and asked her to dance. She looked at me like I was nothing and said coldly with an attitude, "No!" I said, "I was only asking you to dance."

I went back to join Charlie and Donnie who were on another level of the club. Apparently, the word had already gotten around that

Charlie Sheen was in the club that night. This really cute girl came up to the table, looked at the three us and said, "I understand one of you guys was in *Platoon*?" She obviously had no idea who Charlie Sheen was. Without missing a beat, Charlie points to me and said,

> Charlie: Yeah, he did!
> Cute Girl: Really! What was it like? (she was all over me like a cheap suit)
> Me: (improvising) well, uh, you know, it was pretty grueling. We spent a lot of the time in dirty foxholes.
> Cute Girl: (really impressed) Ooooooooh! Really?
> Me: Yeah.

Charlie could barely keep a straight face. This went on for about ten minutes. She really believed I was Charlie Sheen. I'm pretty sure she would have gone home with me until her girlfriend pulled her aside and told her that I wasn't Charlie. That was the end of that. She was so embarrassed, as they left, she turned and gave

Martin Sheen, Charlie Sheen, and Michael Douglas

me a look like I had executed her grandmother. Later on, downstairs, Charlie and I were hanging out at the bar having more tequila shots. The girl I originally asked to dance with earlier, suddenly came up to me with a completely new attitude and said, "Is that Charlie Sheen you're with?" I turned to her and gave her the same cold reception she gave me earlier.

"No!" I said and turned back to Charlie. Paybacks a bitch. By that time it was about 2:00 in the morning and we had to be back on the set at 7:00 am to shoot.

As I was saying goodnight to the guys, one of the waitresses (I'll call her Carla), came over to us. I liked to flirt with Carla whenever I came into the club, but she never seemed interested. Now that I was hanging out with Charlie and working on a major movie, I guess that got her attention. She had just gotten off work and asked what I was doing. I told her that I had to leave because of work in the morning. She whispered in my ear and asked me if I wanted to go home with her (which I did). I guess having celebrity friends really does make a difference. I found out the next day, that Charlie and Donnie had stayed until closing and then went on to a massage parlor and basically stayed up all night.

With a hangover from shooting tequila all night and not getting much sleep at Carla's' place, I staggered onto the set at 7:00 am. After all, I was just a stand-in; I didn't actually have to perform or deliver any lines, I just had to stand there. Charlie was doing the real work as the star of the movie. So I got to the set, and Charlie and Daryl (Hannah) were already on the couch rehearsing for the first scene of the day. Charlie smiled and winked at me and I thought, how did he do it? He stayed up all night drinking tequila and was still able to come to work and perform.

The scene was set and the cameras started rolling, Charlie and Daryl nailed the scene on the first take. If you remember, it's the scene in the film where Charlie finds out that Michael Douglas' character has double-crossed him, and Daryl's character is about to leave him. To drown his pain, Charlie stays up all night drinking tequila. They have a fight. She leaves, and he throws the empty bottle of tequila at the wall, shattering it. Now that's what I call Method Acting! His performance in that scene was stellar! It couldn't have been any more on-the-mark or realistic.

Another cool part of the shoot was the two weeks we spent in South Hampton Long Island. Oliver had rented a beach house, which would serve as Michel Douglas' summer home. There we were, at one of the most beautiful and exclusive beaches on the East Coast. It just so happened that *Rob Lowe* was also in town, starring in a film called *Masquerade*. He came by the set one day and Charlie introduced me to him. (Eight years later, I would co-star with Rob in the spy spoof *Fox Hunt*). Since both film companies were there at the same time, we decided to play a softball game, "Wall Street" versus "Masquerade". We were kicking their ass until *Sean Young* who was playing Michael Douglas' wife in the film; decided she wanted to pitch for our team. Sean was a great actress, but not such a great pitcher. We were winning 26 to 10, and she gave up so many runs that we ultimately lost 29 to 26.

A while later we were filming some exterior scenes near a private school in NYC. I was getting something to drink from the craft service table when all of a sudden I heard a noise. I was not quite sure what it was, but it was getting louder. Suddenly, Charlie comes running around the corner towards me. A moment later a pack of twenty star-struck teenage schoolgirls in matching plaid skirts and white blouses come down the street chasing Charlie. He grabbed me and we jumped inside his trailer not a moment too soon as the girls proceeded to converge on his motor home. It was a good thing I hadn't been mistaken for Charlie at the time or I would have been molested by twenty teenage Catholic schoolgirls.

Charlie: You gotta' help me.
Me: Sure Charlie, whatever you need.
Charlie: I'm NOT HERE! Tell them, I'll give them all an autographed picture, but I won't be able to come out.
Me: Bless you!

So I go outside to face the lust-filled, teenage horde.

Young Girl: Where's Charlie?
Me: (lying through my teeth) Charlie had to leave.
Another Young Girl: Bullshit!
Yet Another Young Girl: We saw him go in there!
Me: Uh, Charlie's not feeling too well right now.
Young Girl: We want Charlie! (They all start to chant in unison)

All The Young Girls: We want Charlie! We want Charlie! We want Charlie!

Me: All Right! All right! Look, Charlie can't come out right now, but he wanted me to give you all signed autograph pictures.

There was a deafening high-pitched collective squeal.
All the Girls: Eeeeee....yay!

I handed out all the pictures and the mob quickly dissipated. As soon as the girls were gone, Charlie got out of his trailer, thanked me, and went home to his apartment.

I was just about to leave as well when another young girl (from the same school) came up to me.

Young Girl: "Oh my gosh, You you looked much younger in Platoon"!

Me: It was good make-up.

Young Girl: The other girls got an autographed picture, could I get one too?

Me: (Not knowing what to say) I'm sorry, I ran out of pictures.

Young Girl: (Really disappointed) Can I at least have your autograph?

Me: (What do I do now?) Sure.

I was in over my head. I figured it would be better to let her think she actually got to meet Charlie than to send her away disappointed that she only got to talk to his stand-in. I signed Charlie's signature the best I could and I handed it to her. She beamed like a little kid on Christmas morning.

Young Girl: Thank you!
Me: You're welcome.
Young Girl: It was nice meeting you!
Me: It was nice meeting you too.

As guilty as I felt doing it, there was a part of me that was just as proud for helping to put a smile on her face. At that moment,

I got to feel what it's like to be a celebrity. I vowed on that day, if I ever got that famous, I would never turn someone down that asked for something as simple as an autograph. There are a lot of celebrities that refuse to sign autographs or talk with their fans. I never understood this small-minded thinking. These same fans are the ones paying at the box office to see them or finance their own independent films on Kick-Starter. Why wouldn't you want to give something back to the fans?

Charlie was always gracious that way. He signed an autograph or picture for any fan that asked for it. Today, I have made tens of thousands of dollars at various Sci-Fi and Horror Conventions around the world signing pictures from different TV shows and movies I've been in. I have never been too busy to sign an autograph or talk to a fan. In fact to this day I still really enjoy it.

Every major actor on Wall Street had their own stand-in. Michael Douglas' stand-in was a New York actor by the name of *Jon Wool*. Since Charlie and Michael worked together a lot on the film, John and I worked together most of the film and became good friends. John was Michaels' stand-in on his previous picture *Fatal Attraction* and was asked to work for him again on *Wall Street*. The term stand-in isn't always accurate. Sometimes, when the director "blocks" out a scene with the actors, the stand-in has to watch the scene and duplicate his or her moves or actions. So there is actually a bit of acting involved because you have to be able to physically play the scene without the dialogue. There is very little actual standing still.

Since John and I were both trained actors and not "professional" extras, we went beyond simply doing the blocking for our respective stars and started learning their lines for each scene. Oliver liked this, because he could get more of an idea about how the scene would play. It got to a point when Oliver would say to us "let's see it"! We would literally act out the scene with dialogue and everything. As I mentioned before, if you do a good job and they like you, there's a good chance they'll throw you a "bone" and give you a part.

In *Wall Street* there is a scene in the trading room where they cut to three or four "trader's" spouting out stock market jargon.

Steve Lim came up to John and I and said that Oliver wanted to give us each a line of dialogue as stockbrokers in Charlie's office. I don't remember what John's line was, but mine was "Circle twenty-nine thousand Niagra's for Templeton"! What was a niagra? And who the hell was Templeton? Luckily, we had several "professional" stock market trader's working on the set as technical advisors. I went over to one of them.

      Me: How's this sound? "Circle twenty-nine thousand Niagra's for Templeton!"
      Technical Advisor: Perfect.
      Me: Really?
      Technical Advisor: Absolutely.
      Me: You sure?
      Technical Advisor: That's how I'd say it.
      Me: Thanks for your help.

I delivered the line with a sense of urgency. I knew enough to know, that time is money in the Stock Market and I knew that when these guys barked out orders, they meant business. They put John and I through make-up and we were ready to go. We each did a couple of takes and then we moved on. Just one line of dialogue meant the difference between stand-in pay of about $120 to $600.00 as a day player. We would also get a screen credit in the film and residuals when the movie was released. To this day, I still receive royalties for *Wall Street* and all the other TV shows and movies I've done over the years.

Jon and I were elated, we were going to be seen talking in Oliver Stone's next film! Well, one of us was anyway. John's line for some reason wound up on the cutting room floor. Unfortunately for John, neither of us found out until the star-studded cast and crew screening. Jon and his wife were sitting directly behind me and my date.

Words cannot describe the anticipation and excitement of seeing my face on the big screen for the first time in a major motion picture. The film started and when it came time for our big scene, I was there but John wasn't. I felt so sorry for him, he was incredibly disappointed (as I would have been), but he seemed to take it well. If it was me, I probably would have broken down and cried.

Another actor that I had the pleasure of working with on *Wall Street* was *James Karen*, who played Charlie's overzealous boss at the trading firm. I had enjoyed James' work on many films including *Poltergeist* and *Return of the Living Dead I & II* (two of my favorite zombie movies of all time). Little did I know it at the time, but "Jimmy" and I would become great friends over the years and I would eventually cast him in the first film that I ever wrote, directed and produced, *Fatal Kiss* which I eventually sold to HBO.

Recently, I got a call from a friend of mine that said he saw me in a re-run of *Wall Street* on cable. That's great I said, that means I'll be getting another royalty check in the mail soon. It's the gift that keeps on giving! You've got to love this business.

Working with Charlie Sheen was great! But my next job would be working with the *Top Gun* star *Tom Cruise*. Two of the biggest movie stars at the time. Things were going pretty good!

Jeff on the Trading Floor in *Wallstreet*

Chapter 9

Cocktail

Several months after we wrapped *Wall Street*, I was still high from the experience of working on an A-List feature film. Since I had worked close to three months on the film, for the first time in

my life, I was financially stable, had money in the bank and didn't have to rush into getting another job other than acting. It wasn't long after that, I got a call from the same casting director from *Wall Street* who said that *Tom Cruise* was coming to New York to shoot a movie called *Cocktail* directed by *Roger Donaldson*. She told them about me and that I just worked with Charlie, so they said okay and hired me based upon her recommendation.

Roger Donaldson was another major league director whose hits include *No Way Out* with *Kevin Costner, Gene Hackman* and *Sean Young* (from *Wall Street*). Roger was a great guy and while we were filming on the NYC streets one night he asked me:

Roger Donaldson: I really like your look Jeff, how come you didn't read for me for a part in this?

Me: I don't know, I'll have to ask my agent that question.

Cocktail production was in town for only eight days because most of the film took place in Jamaica. We were all stoked because that meant we'd be shooting in Jamaica for about two and a half months. Could life get any better? The problem was, we were shooting in the middle of winter in NYC and experiencing one of the coldest winters ever. Unfortunately, unlike *Wall Street* where we shot mostly indoors (in the summer and fall), there were a lot of outdoor scenes and most were at night.

Traditionally, when a production was on a night schedule, your call-time (scheduled start time) would be just before sunset and would go all night for 12-14 hours. In my case, my call time was 6:00 pm and I usually wouldn't wrap until around 8:00 or 9:00 am. This one night was especially cold; it was about 10 degrees below zero with the wind chill factor. We were shooting outdoors near the East River and I literally had to stand in the freezing sub-zero weather while they set up Tom's shots. Unlike *Wall Street* which was pretty easy, I really worked for my money on *Cocktail*. All I could think about was the day when I would be the star and some other poor schmuck would be freezing his ass off standing-in for me.

We finally moved inside a floating club/restaurant that was docked on the river. If you recall in the film, Tom's character brought a bottle of brandy to his on-screen friend *Bryan Brown* that he lost in a bet. So he's outside in the line trying to get inside. I remember I was really tired and hadn't quite gotten used to the all-night shooting schedule. They hadn't needed me for a while, so I fell asleep in one of the back rooms. It was about 3:00 am in the morning when the first A.D. (assistant director) woke me up.

1st A.D: Hey Jeff wake up!
Me: Oh, sorry, are they calling for me?
1st A.D: No, Roger is asking if you wanted to be in the scene.
Me: (still half asleep) What do you mean be in the scene?
1st A.D: In the movie. He wants to know if you want to be in the movie?

Me: What does he want me to do?

1st A.D: (getting impatient) Do you want to do it or not?

Me: (finally getting it) Absolutely!

1st A.D: Then wake up and let's go!

We rushed to the set where everyone was. The cameras were in place, the lighting was done and they were literally waiting to start shooting the next scene. It's a big party scene and there were hundreds of extras. Slightly above the main floor was a second floor with a railing. People were standing at the railing watching the party. Roger saw a guy at the railing with glasses on; he said to the 1st A.D "Get him out of there and put Jeff in his place." We walked over, he pulled the other guy out and put me in his place.

He then introduced me to the female co-star of the film *Kelly Lynch* who played Bryan Brown's girlfriend. Kelly is a beautiful and talented actress that got her start in the business as a high fashion supermodel. Kelly had just come off shooting *Bright Lights, Big City* with *Michael J. Fox* and *Kiefer Sutherland*.

Roger Donaldson: "Kelly this is Jeff, he's going to be in the scene with you.

Kelly Lynch: Great.

Roger Donaldson: You're going to come through the crowd and see Jeff standing at the railing. You guys are old friends, so I want you to come up, give him a kiss and start flirting."

Kelly Lynch: (She looked at me and smiles) Okay.

Roger Donaldson: You got that Jeff?

ME: (Enthusiastically) Yes sir!

Roger Donaldson: Ok, roll sound, cameras…Action!

Kelly comes through the crowd and sees me. She comes up and gives me a kiss. I smile like we're old friends and we started improvising a flirtatious conversation.

Roger Donaldson: Cut! Okay, that was great guys! Let's do it again but this time, Jeff, after you kiss her, I want you to look over at Tom and Bryan and shoot them both a look. Okay?

Me: Yes, sir!

So we did another take, Kelly Kissed me, I shot Tom and Bryan a look and then continued talking to Kelly. We're still rolling and Roger yells out to me "Kiss her again!" So I kiss her again. He then says "Kiss her again" and so I did. This went on for another three times and then Roger finally yelled "Cut!" That was great guys, okay moving on to the next scene."

It was like a whirlwind it happened so fast. I went from sleeping in the back as a stand-in, to being in an important scene of the film kissing *Kelly Lynch*. God, I love this business! Kelly would star opposite *Patrick Swayze* as his love interest in her next film *Roadhouse*. So I guess you can say that I kissed Kelly Lynch before *Patrick Swayze* kissed Kelly Lynch. I wouldn't see Kelly until many years later when I ran into her at *Danny Devito's* 4th of July party at his home in Malibu. I reminded her of our scene in *Cocktail* and we both laughed. Even today people call me up and say, Hey Jeff, I just saw you in *Cocktail*!"

Unfortunately, close to the end of the New York shoot, we

were notified that the local stand-ins and some of the crew would not be going to Jamaica in order to cut the production costs. They would hire Jamaican locals to do our jobs once they got in town. From a production standpoint, it made sense, they wouldn't have to fly us in, pay us a daily per-diem (food expense money), hotel accommodations, etc. My upcoming paid vacation to Jamaica had just been canceled. I was now going to be stuck in New York

City for the rest of the extremely harsh winter. The best laid plans of Mice and Men.

I was pretty bummed. Although I was not going to be spending the winter in the sun, sand and tropical waters of Jamaica, I was carefully crafting a plan to leave New York for good and move back to California. Part of that plan was making a lot of money over the next few months on *Cocktail* in order to move back to LA in style, as opposed to moving back without much money and starting from scratch.

Well, that particular door was shut but I was about to embark on an adventure that most men (and women) can only dream about. It would be a relationship with Playboy that would span the next 20 years.

Chapter 10

I Was a Playboy Rabbit

Having worked at the some of the most reputable restaurants and Hotels in NYC by this time, I had quite an impressive resume' (as far as waiters go). By this time my twin brother Jerry had also moved to New York to seek his fame and fortune. The good news was, we could work the twin act together and have better opportunities for commercials and modeling. At the time *Hugh Hefner* was no longer running *Playboy Enterprises,* and his daughter *Christie Hefner* was put in charge of the day-to-day corporate operations in Los Angeles. The New York Playboy club had closed several years earlier and there was talk of re-opening a brand new Club in the city, but Christie didn't want to open up just another Playboy Men's Club. Her idea was to open a spectacular New York City Nightclub that would attract and cater to both men and women. The targeted market would be successful and affluent New Yorkers and celebrities. To make this happen, Christie decided to create a new brand and not only have female Playboy Bunnies, but to add attractive and sexy men (Playboy Rabbits) to the mix to provide eye-candy for the women as well.

Famed Restaurateur *Richard Mellman* was hired to create this unique and ground breaking new Nightclub in the city. His company *Lettuce Entertain You Enterprises*, is a Chicago-based corporation that owns more than 100 restaurants nationwide, many of which had specific themes from the menu to the décor. When Mellman came to New York to create the Playboy Empire Club, he brought years of experience with him. The first thing Richard needed to find were Bunnies and Rabbits.

Actors, dancers, singers and just about every good-looking guy and gal in the three boroughs came in to apply.

At the time, *Chippendale's* (an all male dance revue) was still a big sensation and had a very popular show in New York. Needless to say, they were the first guys to line up for an interview to be the first ever Playboy Rabbits. But Playboy and Mellman had other ideas. They weren't looking for Chippendale's "male strippers"; they wanted attractive, upscale and classy men and women that were good waiters and servers, not "cheesecake." Word went out to all the talent agencies looking for model types with waiting, hosting and bartending experience. Needless to say my twin brother Jerry and I were interviewed. They were impressed with the fact that we had such a well-rounded upbringing. Having grown up in both Michigan (with Midwestern values) and the west coast in Los Angeles with a "Hollywood" background.

The Philadelphia Inquirer
people/home/entertainment   Monday, November 11, 1985

Playboy Club in N.Y. hears one complaint: Male bunnies wear too much.

The traditional bunny costume still lives, but there are some variations nowadays.

Rich Mellman surrounded by the Playboy Rabbits

Part of the training to be a Bunny was learning the famous "Bunny Dip," where the bunnies (who all had ample cleavage), would dip their legs down when serving, instead of bending over with

81

their cleavage or rears in the customers face. That's one example of how Playboy was a class act and was respectful of both women and the clubs customers. It was one of the things that I liked most about Hef and the entire Playboy Organization. He respected the women in and out if his magazine and only tastefully showed so much of a Playmate's "perfect" body in all of his centerfolds. Other competing magazines like *Hustler* and *Easy Rider* showed everything (and I mean everything), and to me that wasn't sexy, it was sleazy.

When I was kid, I grew up reading three magazines, *National Lampoon, Mad Magazine* and of course *Playboy*. After all, *Playboy Magazine* was a young man's foray into manhood. Those unforgettable images of the most beautiful women in the world in a variety of enticing poses, gave us all the fantasy that one day we would have a Playmate for a girlfriend or better yet, a wife. I did have the former for a while which was pretty great, another childhood dream come true. Anyway, back to the Empire Club.

The design of the Bunny and Rabbit "outfits" was the biggest challenge. They wanted the men to look sexy, but classy. Style was an utmost concern. The last thing they wanted was for the guys to look like they were from Chippendale's. So a shirtless black tuxedo with classic Playboy white cuffs (complete with Playboy cuff links) and a Playboy white collar with a black bow tie was "the look." Since my twin brother and I were athletic, we were initially dressed as "Tennis Rabbits." We wore white pleated pants, white loafers,

white sleeveless tennis sweaters with the "Rabbit cuffs" and "Rabbit collars" and black bow tie. The wardrobe designer then had the idea to sew a large black letter "P" on the front of my sweater and the letter "B" on the front of Jerry's sweater so that when we stood next to each other it read, "PB" for Playboy.

The Bunnies were easier to dress since the classic Playboy Bunny outfit was already a trademark of the club and branding. What was decided was, to take the classic bunny outfit and make it more creative as a new, original, themed bunny character. The new "character Bunnies" would be defined by the women wearing them. For example, a woman of Asian descent became a Geisha Bunny, a female bodybuilder was an Olympic Bunny, and so on. Some of the

other Bunny costumes were themed as a Bride, Chef, Cupid, *Madonna* (the singer, not the biblical character) and of course, because we were in New York, there was a Statue of Liberty Bunny.

Playboy Bunnies at The Empire Club

Finally, we were all trained, dressed and ready for action. The Opening Night of the Playboy Empire Club was the hottest ticket in town and everybody wanted in. Because of the club's size, the guest list was limited to the top celebrities, New York elite and A-Listers which included Fortune 500 magnate, *Malcolm Forbes*. I served a couple of drinks to actor *Tony Danza* (star of the hit TV show *Who's the Boss?*) who tipped me forty dollars. I thought, "I'm going to love this job!"

The Opening Night was a huge success, and The Rabbits had

made their official inaugural appearance.

Pictures of us (and the new Bunnies) went nationwide to all the news services. We were in *People Magazine*, *The New York Times*, and had a featured article in the March 1986 issue of *Playboy Magazine* with actress *Sally Field* on the cover dressed in a black sequined Playboy Bunny outfit. I have to say, she was pretty hot back then. There was a picture of Hef in the Empire Club surrounded by all the Bunnies and Rabbits. Instantly, we

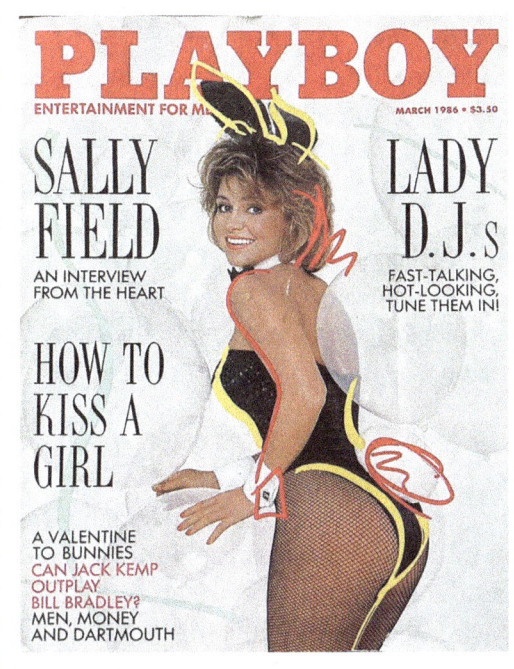

Sally Field **as a Playboy Bunny**

were worldwide celebrities. Being a Playboy Bunny or Rabbit certainly had its perks. Bunnies were topped in prestige only by the actual Playboy Playmates (some of which were also Bunnies back in the day and vise-versa).

The Bunnies and Rabbits would be requested for personal appearances at everything from Charity Events to the US Tennis Open in Flushing Meadows. We would get extra money for these appearances and be driven in either a Limousine or by a Private Town Car. We were celebrities and were treated like royalty (which Playboy insisted upon). By that time, everybody in NY knew who we were. If we needed tickets to a Broadway Show, dinner reservations at any of the top restaurants, or immediate entry into any of the popular nightclubs, we had carte blanche. Needless to say, when we weren't working, we were partying and having the time of our lives.

Working for Playboy was different than anything I had ever experienced. The general rule for most corporate waiter or bartender jobs was no fraternization with the customers or other employees or it could be grounds for termination. I once had relations with my manager (I'll call her Dana) when I worked for the *Omni Hotel*. She was extremely sexy and kept pretending that she wasn't interested in me, until I finally talked her into having a cocktail after work one night. After several martinis, she confessed that she always liked me, but was afraid that if we went out she could lose her job that she worked so hard to get. I told her as far as I was concerned, if we were together, it would be no one's business but our own. We went home together that night and were together for the next six months. She was extremely conservative and all business at work, but in the bedroom, she was anything but.

I left the Omni (breakfast and lunch shift), and moved next door to the dinner shift at the French Brasserie that was also part of the Hotel. The gourmet French menu was a lot more expensive, and catered to a European crowd looking for that type of cuisine that wasn't readily available in the city. Dana and I continued to see each other without any fallout at work. A lot of times, a bunch of the staff would go across the street to have drinks after our shift. Dana and I would play it off that we were just friends. I think people started to realize that we were together, because we would conveniently share a cab ride home from the bar together every time. I actually confided in one of my best friends Eddie, who initially helped me get me the job. When I told him, his jaw hit the floor, because every guy fantasized about her. Every guy that hit on her, would be blown off and told that she had a boyfriend (which was secretly me).

While I was used to keeping my work and my private life separate, at the Playboy Empire Club, we were actually encouraged to fraternize with the guests and interact with them, including dancing if we wanted as long as it didn't get in the way of our service duties. What man or women wouldn't want to go to a Playboy Club where you could dance with a Bunny or a Rabbit. That being said, we weren't allowed to date any of the staff as that could make for an uneasy work environment if things didn't work out. Nobody complained, there was already so much action going on with our friends and their friends and regular customers that we got to know, that it was just one big party! And the best part was, we were getting paid to do it.

After about nine months, as with any new club in the city, the novelty started to wear off and the club managers were trying different things in order to keep things new and exciting. They decided to switch from a set dinner menu to an all-you-can-eat buffet, which was amazing. As you can imagine, we had one of the top chefs in town and the food was magnificent! Not only that, with a buffet, we didn't need to take any food orders, just drinks. We would still have assigned tables and cater to the guests with the buffet on their dinner check, so even though we didn't have to serve the food, we still got tipped on the overall check.

Hanging with a couple of Bunnies

We were making even more money in tips than we had ever before. It was the first job in my life that I actually looked forward to going to work every day.

Always the idea man, I came up with a concept for certain nights at the club to have a theme. At the time, one of the top Night Clubs in New York was called *Club Area, The Area* or just *Area*.

Once a month, the club changed their theme. They not only had their employees all dress with the theme, they completely redecorated the entire club with that theme every single month. I don't know how much it cost them to do it, but it was packed every night of the week and made it cool and different, so it literally was a different club from month to month which kept it fresh. One week it could be a futuristic world, another week it might be a jungle theme and once when Ten Mile Island was a hot topic, it was decorated as an Atomic Power Plant, with flashing red lights, radioactive warning signs on the walls and employees in Hazmat Suits serving cocktails with glowing faux ice cubes so the drink looked like it was radioactive. They really went all out.

I suggested that we have something similar, different theme nights at the club, and since I was an actor and had a lot of costumes in my closet, I would be the host and one or two of the bunnies would be part of it. They would then rent the costumes for the bunnies and some props and dress one of the rooms in that theme. We had a historical explorer theme where I wore an Indiana Jones type outfit. One of the bunnies dressed like a jungle girl and my brother Jerry talked them into renting a full Gorilla costume that he wore.

Jeff tames some Bunnies on Jungle Night

We would take Polaroid pictures with the guests and charge them a fee to keep the picture. Another theme was similar, where I was an archaeologist and one of the bunnies was Cleopatra, we had a pyramid and everything.

Cleopatra Queen of Denial

My favorite (and was a big hit) was the *James Bond* theme. I was dashing in my double-breasted tuxedo as Bond with several of the bunnies as Bond Girls.

We served martinis (shaken not stirred) and had a few gambling tables set up to look like *Casino Royale*. I got paid a flat rate for the night and all I had to do was spout famous lines from the Bond films and take pictures with the patrons. Those were some of my happiest memories at the Empire Club.

The Bunnies and Rabbits make a personal appearance

Shortly after that Jerry and I decided to take a trip back to LA to see our friends (and to make them jealous of our new found fame). We were in town for a week when I got the bright idea to call Playboy and see if we could get invited to the Playboy Mansion. I called the corporate headquarters and was transferred to several different people, until I was connected directly to someone at the mansion. I told him who we were, that we were Rabbits at the New York Empire Club and that we were only in town for a short period of time. He said that he would check and get back to me.

As promised, I got a call back saying that they would love to invite us up to the mansion for a quick tour. Quick tour? Well, we thought a quick tour is better than nothing at all. He said he would check the dates and get back to me, which he did. He said that Hef was having one of his screening parties on Sunday Night at 6:00pm and would we like to come to the mansion for dinner and a movie. Would we? WooHoo! We were given the address in Holmby Hills, a very exclusive area near Westwood. As you might imagine, every home is a mansion in Holmby Hills, but there is only one Playboy Mansion.

At 6:01pm we drove to the address. At the entrance to the

driveway were two large wrought iron gates (you just didn't drive up to the Playboy Mansion). Just before the gate to the left was an intercom system. I pressed the button.

The World Famous Playboy Mansion at sunset

Security: May I help you?

Me: Yes, Jeff and Jerry Rector here for movie night...

Security: (He paused as he looked at the guest list) Okay, come up the driveway to the main house.

Me: Thank you.

The two large gates swung open and we drove up an incredibly long and steep driveway that led up to the main house. When we came around the final bend, we could see the Mansion coming up before us. It was even more grand and luxurious than any pictures I had previously seen. Directly in front of the mansion was a beautiful circular driveway with an enormous fountain in the middle. There were several Valet Parking Attendants waiting to park our car, (of course). We entered the front door of the mansion and were immediately greeted by several staff members welcoming us and ushering us into one of the many elegant and beautifully decorated rooms in the estate. There was a bar set-up with a staff bartender and an enormous hand-carved antique table with an amazing assortment of food (buffet style) with succulent prime fillets, seafood, salads, side dishes and desserts.

We ponied up to the bar to get a cocktail. As we were sipping a cool delicious libation, we began to take in the room. There were about 20 people so far, 6 or 7 were guys and the rest were Playboy Playmates. Hef was nowhere in sight, (he hadn't come downstairs yet). Most of the guests for any of the parties are either celebrities or personal friends of Hef's. We felt extremely honored and overwhelmed at the same time, but the cocktails definitely helped. Two guys came over and introduced themselves, they were *Vince Van Patten* and his brother *Jimmy*. Although they weren't twins like us, they were close in age and looked very similar. Vince and Jimmy were both actors and teen idols. Vince would later marry beautiful Soap Star *Eileen Davidson*, who would win an Emmy Award and become one of the *Real Housewives of Beverly Hills* on the hit Bravo TV series.

Many years later I would become the President and Festival Director for the *Burbank International Film Festival*. One year we screened a sci-fi film starring *Eileen Davidson* and I was contacted by Bravo and asked if *The Real Housewives of Beverly Hills* could attend the festival. Hell Yeah! You can't pay for that kind of incredible worldwide publicity. In fact, I was featured in two episodes of the show, where I met and talked to *Lisa Vanderpump* as well as interviewed Eileen on the festival red carpet.

Back at the Mansion, I told Vince and Jimmy I had just come from New York for a short visit and was going back soon. They were really great guys, we had some laughs and they introduced us to some of the Playmates. We all dined on the incredible food and relaxed in the movie room, (a private screening room for about 30 people). We nestled into the plush leather couches and a couple of Playmates cozied up to Jerry and I. They thought it is was cute that we were identical twins and that we were Rabbits. One of the girls started kissing my neck and put her hand on my leg. Just before the film started, Hef arrived with two of the most beautiful playmates there (of course) and they sat down on the main couch together.

We found out that Hef would host these Screening Parties every Sunday evening. A lot of times, Hef would screen a major motion picture before it was even released to the public. It was kind of surreal; part of me still couldn't believe I was actually there. After the film ended, Hef went back upstairs with some of the girls and the rest of us continued to eat and drink. Around midnight, the party was pretty much over and we made our way outside to get our cars. I gave my new Playmate friend my NY phone number (cell phones and the internet were not yet available) and she wasn't allowed to give out the Mansion private phone number. Since she and most of the Playmates that were there that night actually lived at the Mansion, that was the end of the evening. I kissed her goodbye and

Hugh Heffner at the Opening Night of The Empire Club

we drove off into the night. Another childhood dream had just come true and I was just getting started.

After returning to New York, we went back to work at the Playboy Club. At this point, we had reached rock-star status having partied at the Playboy Mansion. Several years later, I would become a regular guest at the mansion for most of the major parties.

As we would all soon come to realize, the Empire Club in all it's glory would unfortunately be short-lived. Attendance started to dwindle, other clubs like Studio 54, Club Area and Sanctuary (which was actually a Catholic church turned into a nightclub), were stealing the business from the Playboy Club. As was traditional in NYC, clubs usually lasted only 6 months before the party crowd moved onto the next new hip club. We actually lasted more than a year.

The news was devastating, we had become a family and the family was about to be split up. Where would we go? What would we do? How do you follow up a gig with Playboy?

I wasn't about to go back to working at Tavern-on-the Green. So I made the only logical decision. Said goodbye to my agent, my friends and go back to Los Angeles. But not before a few goodbye parties! The last month was crazy, word got out that the club was closing and everybody and their brother wanted to be there before it was gone forever. Business was never better. We encouraged all of our friends to come in and it was one big party.

We found out that the Bunnies were going to rent two adjoining suites at the famous *Ritz-Carlton Hotel* and have a girls going away "lingerie slumber party."

After discovering what floor they were on, I talked the other Rabbits (and management) into renting a suite right down the hall. Hatching a plan to crash their Bunny party.

I had just started seeing someone new that I met at the club and she wanted to be part of the fun, so we checked into the Suite early to bring in the booze and set up the bar. We were there early and alone, so we decided to take advantage of the king-sized bed.

Since the girls were going to be in lingerie and pajamas, the guys decided to be in boxers and underwear for the big surprise.

Not to be outdone, my sexy new girlfriend was in lingerie as well, to be in the spirit of things. She was the only woman in the guys Suite as we were about to crash the all-girl slumber party. Guys started showing up an hour or so later and we all started doing shots. As the ladies were getting liquored up in their suite, we were getting primed ourselves. About 10:00pm we were pretty lit and decided to make the move down the hall.

A buddy of mine, Kevin, had a Hotel waiters jacket from his years at another hotel and it looked perfect. We found a room-service cart with a plate and cover on it and wheeled it down the hall to the girls' door. What a sight, 25 guys in their underwear lined up on either side of the door armed with champagne and assorted bottles of liquor. We were set for the attack. Military trained special force commandos weren't as prepared as we were. Kevin knocked on the door. Anyone of the bunnies looking through the peephole would only see Kevin outside with a room service cart, Hotel Jacket, white shirt and bow tie. They couldn't see below the cart, to see that he was only wearing underwear.

Knock! Knock!
One of the bunnies: Who's there?
Kevin: Room Service.
One of the Bunnies: But we didn't order anything.
Kevin: (Thinking quickly) It's complimentary from the manager...
One of the Bunnies: Just a minute...
From inside, we could hear her talking to the other girls.
One of the bunnies: He said it's from management...
One of the other bunnies: Well, let him in.

We could barely contain our laughter, as we were all three sheets-to-the-wind by this point. She unlocked the door and opened it.
Kevin: Good evening ladies!

As he wheeled the cart inside the room, we all suddenly stormed in behind him. The girls screamed, as they were caught off guard by the masterful execution of our ambush. The screams quickly turned to squeals of delight, as they were as drunk as we were and decided to go with the flow. Because we all knew each other and liked each other, everyone started grabbing everyone else. It was a melee of drunken proportions. One of the guys brought in a Boom Box and started playing dance music. Everyone started doing shots, which fueled the revelry even more. The rest is kind of a blur, but an hour or so later; there was a knock at the door.

Knock. Knock.
No answer.
(Even harder) Knock! Knock!
Still no answer.

Knock! Knock! Knock! (More like, pound! pound! pound!)
Security: Hotel Security...Open the door!

Honestly with the music and laughter and everything else, we barely heard anyone at the door. One of the buzzed bunnies finally opens the door. The security guard bursts in. You can imagine the look on his face; it looked like a scene from "Caligula."

Security: We've received numerous noise complaints.
One of the Bunnies: We're just having a little party. Want a drink?
Security: That wouldn't be appropriate.
Me: I'm sure we're not the only people partying in the hotel. Listen, we all worked for Playboy, the club just closed and this may be the last time most of us will ever see each other again.

The security guard was taking in all the scantily clad bunnies. One of the girls went over and started flirting with him.

One of the Bunnies: Can't we just have a little party? We promise to behave ourselves...

The security looked around and decided to give us a warning.

Security: All right, but you'll have to turn the music down and if I get any more complaints, I'm going to have to shut it down.

The bunny hugged him and we all thanked him for being a nice guy. Unfortunately, about an hour later, a hotel guest reported seeing someone running down the hallway naked. That was it.

Knock. Knock.
No answer.
(Even harder) Knock! Knock!
Still no answer.
Knock! Knock! Knock! (More like, pound! pound! pound!)
Security: Hotel Security...Open up!
One of the bunnies once again opens the door. This time, there is a three-person hotel security team.

Head of Security: Okay, that's it the parties over.

Me: What are you talking about; we turned the music down like you requested...

Head of Security: That was before we got several complaints about people running naked through the hallways...

Me: Oh...well, how do you know it was us?

Head of Security: (looking at a room filled with drunken half-naked people) Really?

Me: Okay. We'll be good I promise...

Head of Security: It's too late for that, in fact, I'm going to have to ask everyone to gather their belongings and leave the hotel.

Me: You're kicking us out? We paid for three Suites...

Head of Security: Once you're out, if we determine that there is no damage to any of the rooms or any property, we will give you a refund.

Me: You can't do that, we have rights...

Head of Security: You either leave peacefully, or we will contact NYPD and let them handle it. Guys, lets go, return to your room and pack up your things...

One of the Rabbits: Okay. Listen girls, we'll call you in a few minutes and we'll figure where we're going to continue the party.

Bunnies: (in unison) Yay!

I grabbed some of the booze and me and my girl jumped in a cab. As far as we were concerned, the party was over and we wanted to get busy back at my place. I never knew where everybody went or what happened after that. But as predicted, everyone went their own way. As quickly as we had all been brought together at the club when we were hired, we separated just as quickly. I would never see most of those people ever again. It was a fitting end for a fantastic ride with a wonderful cast and crew.

Thank you *Rich Mellman*, and *Christie Hefner* for including us in this amazing and unique piece of Playboy history. I will always be honored and grateful for the opportunity of working with you.

PLAYBOY'S EMPIRE CLUB

The Rabbits—boy Bunnies!—were the hottest copy when Playboy's Empire Club welcomed the world in November, but almost everything was new at New York's most colorful playpen. There were Bunnies— Theme Bunnies!—one, minus an ear, in the gallery near the Van Gogh. Some of the press was catty. "Note the Yuppies at the bar," wrote one Peggy Landers. Hey, we *like* Yuppies. The number-one Rabbit (above) presided, emerging from comfy Mansion West to renew his firm commitment to a good time.

Diane Sawyer took a few ticks off from *60 Minutes* to chat with Hef (above). At the Club (right), Manhattanites hopped in to see what all the noise was about and caught a glimpse of Catherine Bach (below), who showed up without the Dukes but was a Hazzard to traffic.

Mr. Money, Malcolm Forbes, met Bunny Belinda (above) and smiled as widely as you would if you had his wealth. George Plimpton (below) arrived on his bicycle to meet with Christie. We're hoping George will don an open-breasted tux for a new first-person report, *I, Rabbit.*

A Page from Playboy Magazine featuring the opening of the club

Chapter 11

Escape From New York

New York was exciting and fun, but it was time to return to the ocean, constant sunshine, and bikini-clad California Girls. I paid my dues, added some new acting credits to my resume, and had

Jeff on the streets of New York in *The Chinatown Murders*

some money in my pocket. It was now finally time to return home to Los Angeles.

As I carefully finalized my plans for my grand departure from New York, I "was cast" as the lead in a film called *The Chinatown Murders*. It was written and directed by some Chinese filmmaker whose name escapes me. I don't remember if it was a feature film

97

since we only shot for six days. I play a New York detective who gets partnered with a young cop from China to solve a murder involved with the local drug trade. All that I remember about it was that I got paid, and the director said I did a great job. To this day, I've never seen the film and don't know if it ever got released or even finished, but it was one of my first stepping stones to climbing the tall ladder in Hollywood and I was grateful for the work as always

Back in LA I got an apartment in North Hollywood. It was great reconnecting with everyone I hadn't seen or even talked to in over 5 years. I got back into the swing of things pretty quickly, and some of my old friends, like me, had also moved up in the world.

The LA scene raged with a party in the Hollywood Hills every other night. I started dating again, but after my disappointing relationships in New York, I wasn't in a hurry to jump into a new one. Los Angeles, as you can imagine, has some of the most beautiful women in the nation, and every actress, dancer, or singer has come from all over to seek their fortune in Hollywood.

As New York City mostly catered to theater, commercials, and modeling, Hollywood was the mecca for television and motion pictures. Anyone interested in being a TV or movie star came to Los Angeles, not New York. I was young, single, and focused on my acting career, not getting married or starting a family. Friends of mine did go the family route, but pretty soon, when they weren't earning enough money in acting to support a wife and kids, they were pretty quickly convinced to "get a real job" to bring home the bacon.

I've seen many friends (both men and women) give up their dreams to make a spouse happy and to be a good provider. That wasn't me. My career always came first, and I was always very upfront about it with anyone I was dating. Current statistics show that it costs an average family $233,610 to raise a child from birth until their seventeenth birthday. That's $14,000 a year per child. That's a lot of oatmeal and cornflakes, which didn't fit into my operating budget.

Now that I was back in LA, I needed to find a new agent to keep my acting career going. Being gone for five years meant starting from scratch again. My previous agent was no longer in the business and I needed to get new representation as soon as possible. Because of all my work in New York, my resume had considerably more credits than when I first moved from LA. I searched the Talent Agency listings and found a very reputable Theatrical Agent that represented actors for both film and television.

I picked up the phone and called them; a receptionist answered informing me that to be considered for representation I should send them my current head shot and resume and that they would be in touch if they were interested ("Don't call us, we'll call you"). So I did and a few days later, I got a call saying they wanted to meet me. I met with the head of the agency (I don't remember his name) and we had a nice conversation. I shared my dreams and aspirations and thanked him for taking time out of his busy day to meet me. If it sounds like I was brown-nosing him, I was.

He looked at my head shot and said that it was excellent, that I was very handsome. I didn't know where this was going, but I said, "Thank you." He turned over my picture and started looking over my resume. He saw the film credits for *Wall Street* and *Cocktail* and my NYC theatre credits, including an off-off Broadway show.

> Here's how it works in New York. If you were in a primary Broadway production, you were "On Broadway"; if you were in a smaller production off one of the side streets from Broadway, you were considered "Off-Broadway" if you were in any other production anywhere else in the city, your production was "Off-Off-Broadway." That was me. But I didn't care because I was more interested in TV and film than in theatre; however, if you lived in New York and were an actor, dancer, or singer, theatre was the thing to a Hollywood Agent!

He finished looking at my resume and said, "Oh, a New York actor, I'd love to work with you!" And that was it. I had a new agent.

Let me put this in context. In the entertainment business, Los Angeles has always had the reputation of having the most "Beautiful people" but not necessarily the most talented. If you were an actor from New York (it didn't matter what you looked like), you were respected as a good actor. So I had to leave LA, go to New York, and then go back to LA before I got any respect as an actor.

My new agent was great; he was sending me out a lot, and I was booking many roles and getting close to booking others, when, all of a sudden, I wasn't getting sent out at all. It was perplexing, but in show business, nothing is guaranteed. I enjoyed having some free time off to play golf, go to the beach, and enjoy sunny California.

I was at a party one night, and I ran into a friend named Mike; he was also with my agent, so I asked, hey Mike, how's it going? He said great. I just switched to a new agent and booked a big commercial.

I said, "That's great, congratulations! But why did you leave our agent? The last time we talked, we both agreed he was doing an excellent job for us." Mike said, what are you talking about? He died of a heart attack a month ago. I said, "Wow, no wonder I hadn't heard from him." Nobody from the agency had bothered to let me know when the funeral was, let alone that he had died in the first place. He was nice and had worked hard for me; I would have liked to have paid my respects at his funeral.

It reminded me of a joke: A guy calls his agent, and the receptionist answers the phone and says, "Bernie Schwartz Agency?" the client says, "Can I speak to Bernie Schwartz, please?" The receptionist says, "Oh, I'm sorry, Bernie Schwartz died...". The client says, "Oh, okay..." and hangs up. A few minutes later, the client calls back, and the receptionist answers the phone and says," Bernie Schwartz Agency?" the client says, "Can I speak to Bernie Schwartz, please?" The receptionist says, "Oh, I'm sorry, Bernie Schwartz died...". The client says, "Oh, okay..." and hangs up. A few minutes later, the client calls back again; the receptionist answers the phone and says, "Bernie Schwartz Agency?" the client says, "Can I speak to Bernie Schwartz, please?" The receptionist says, "Look, don't you get it! Bernie Schwartz is dead!" the client says, "yeah, I get it, I just love hearing you say it!"

Chapter 12

The Los Angeles Playboy Club

I still had some money in the bank and I was auditioning, but I needed to get a steady job to keep from going through my savings from the Playboy Empire Club until I could get a new agent and start acting again. Fortunately, a friend offered me a job. I'd be working with him in the mail room for one of the top law offices located in Century City, a modern, high-end business district bordering Beverly Hills, with expensive hotels and offices on one end and *Twentieth Century Fox Studios* at the other end.

Century City's landmark at the time was the *ABC*

Entertainment Center, a complex with two five-story office buildings, a limestone plaza, several fountains, and two tall, gleaming Twin Towers (that resemble the Twin Towers in New York City that were destroyed by the terrorist attack on 9/11). The Center also had a movie theater, fine-dining restaurants, and the famous *Shubert Theater*, a 2,100-seat show house where attendees could see Broadway-level productions, concerts, and A-List performers. It was also the location of the *LA Playboy Club*.

The majestic *Shubert Theatre* opened in 1972 with a production of *Follies* directed by *Harold Prince* and *Michael Bennett*. In its 30-year history, the theatre hosted productions

The Schubert Theatre - a former LA Landmark

including *A Chorus Line*, *Les Misérables*, *Cats*, *Evita*, *Sunset Boulevard*, *Dreamgirls*, *Ragtime*, *Beauty and the Beast*, the sell-out production of *Momma Mia,* and the 1990 *Miss Universe pageant.* It had previously hosted the *Emmy Awards* in 1973 and 1976. The theatre closed in January 2002 due to a lack of bookings and was demolished to make way for a $285 million office building. When the Shubert Theatre closed, I remember thinking; "My God, this is one of the few significant theaters Los Angeles still has. " It was a bad sign that the LA entertainment industry landscape was indeed changing, and not in a good way.

My new job at the Law firm was super easy: distributing the mail in the morning, collecting it, and sorting it in the afternoon. The pay was good, I got to wear nice clothes, and everyone in the office was super friendly. However, a problem arose soon after when my buddy was reprimanded for being constantly late to work and had a less than enthusiastic attitude toward the job itself. I asked him if we had to be concerned about being fired, and he said no, don't worry about it. So I didn't. I just kept showing up for work and doing the job every day, whether he was there or not.

One morning, I got called into the head lawyer's office. He told me to close the door, which I did. "Have a seat." he said. I sit down. There is an awkward silence. I couldn't stand the pressure anymore, so I said, "Did I do something wrong?" There was another awkward silence and he said, "No, we just fired your buddy today, and we'd like you to take over his position as head of the mail room. "Oh," I said, an intense wave of relief washing over my entire body. "Does that mean I'll be getting a raise?" I asked confidently. "No, but we like you, which is why we're keeping you on." "Of course," I said, "I really appreciate that!" "Okay, then, just keep doing the job you're doing." "Thank you, sir!" I get up and get out of there as quickly as possible. Whew! That was a close one, I thought. I'm now running the mail room for one of the top law offices in Century City. It wasn't my dream job, but hey, it was better than waiting tables.

The LA Playboy Club was located just below the Shubert Theatre on the lower level, which made the location private to the public eye. The actual club entrance was hidden around a corner, so you would only know to look for it if you knew it was there, part of Hef's plan for privacy and exclusivity. At the entrance was a neon sign with the iconic Playboy logo with the rabbit and ears, no signage that said the Playboy Club, just the illuminated logo. Classy but mysterious. The club opened around 11:00am for lunch and stayed open until 2:00am.

Having previously been employed at the *New York Playboy Empire Club*, I missed the fun and excitement that the Playboy clubs offered. Since I was a former Playboy Rabbit, I was welcomed with open arms as a new member of the LA club, which also made me a celebrity at both the club and in Playboy's intimate social circles. Since working in the East Tower of the ABC Entertainment Center, I loved attending the club for lunch, dinner, and drinks. It was also an impressive place to schmooze entertainment industry people as I hoped they would hire me as an actor.

Soon, everyone at the club knew me, and I became a popular regular. The Playboy bunnies were all beautiful and sophisticated because that was Playboy's standard. You couldn't just be attractive with a great body; you had to be smart, friendly, and have goals and aspirations beyond being a Bunny. One day, I was flirting with one of the Bunnies, and she asked where I worked. I said I was in one of the Law offices in the East Tower. "Ooh," she says; I wasn't about to tell her now that I was working in the mail room. I asked if she wanted to go out sometime, but she said there was a strict policy that the Bunnies could not date any club members. That was certainly not the mandate when I worked in the New York Club. Rabbits and Bunnies were all dating club patrons, and we were having the time of our lives.

The original *Los Angeles Playboy Club* was founded by Hugh Hefner in 1964 and located in West Hollywood at 8560 Sunset Boulevard (the world-famous *Sunset Strip*). I would soon be picked up by the *Playboy Modeling Agency* housed in that building as one of their featured male actors and models.

Playboy Enterprises owned the 10-story building, with the club taking up the first four floors. On the weekend nights, the lines were around the block. Hefner lived on the top floor, inside a penthouse that was very James Bond, very top secret. You could push a button, and an entire wall would slide away to reveal the bar. He even had a round bed up there. All the accouterments that every Rat Pack pretender only dreamed of were happening in Hefner's club and inside Hefner's bedroom on the Sunset Strip.

In 1968, Hefner premiered his television show, *Playboy After Dark,* which was taped around the corner at the CBS studios on Fairfax Avenue.

"Every night after the show, there was a party upstairs in Hefner's penthouse, the likes of which those poor lonely saps downstairs at the bar, swilling their 007 martinis, could only dream of," the *Los Angeles Times* said in a 1996 story.

Club-goers would come for the Bunnies, attired in their signature outfits with bunny ears and cottontails augmented with collars, cuffs, and bow ties but stayed for the top-level comedians and musicians. The Playboy Club was far more than the *Hooters* of its day. It married cultural savvy and showbiz glitz. Comedians who played at the club included *Shecky Green, David Brenner, Rich Little, Jerry Van Dyke*, and *Lily Tomlin*, as well as musicians *Sonny Rollins* and *Al Jarreau*. Actress and singer *Lainie Kazan* oversaw the Los Angeles branch, also known as *Lainie's Room*, where she was the only woman to run a Playboy Club until *Christie Hefner* created the *Playboy Empire Club* almost twenty years later. When the vibrant rock and roll scene of the late 1960s was over, Hefner moved the club and the rest of his empire's operations to Century City in 1972.

Things were going pretty well for me; I was back in sunny California, had a good, steady job and was a popular member of the Playboy Club. I was the envy of all my male friends, and as far as everyone else knew, I had a respectable white-collar job in Century City. Everything was pretty good, pretty, pretty, pretty good, as *Larry David* would say on *Curb Your Enthusiasm*.

One day, I was having lunch at *McCormack and Schmick's*, a popular upscale restaurant at The *ABC Entertainment Center*. I struck up a conversation with another businessman wearing a suit; his name was *Bob Shock*. It turned out that Bob worked at one of the top advertising agencies located in the East Tower.

I told him that my father also worked in advertising as an art director. We had a few laughs and had lunch together. He asked what I did. I told him that I was an actor, but I was currently working at a law firm. "What are you doing there?" He asked; after an awkward moment, I said I was running the mail room. "What do you do at the ad agency?" I asked, and he said, "I'm running the mail room." We had a big laugh over that one.

He asked if I had thought about making a change. "What do you mean?" "You won't stay at the Law Firm forever, will you?" "Of course not, just until my acting career takes off." "How would you like to work in an ad agency?" "Doing what?" "Running the mail room." "Isn't that you're job?" "It is, but I have an opportunity to work in accounts, which is where I want to be. I can move up the ladder if I can find a suitable replacement." "What are you saying?" "I'm saying that you'd be perfect if you're willing to make a change." "I don't know, I've only been there four months, and they've been really good to me." "Wouldn't you rather work in the entertainment industry?" "Well, sure, but how do we know they'll hire me?" "I'll talk to them." "You'll have to come in for an interview, of course, but they'll love you." "How much does it pay?" "More than they're giving you at the law offices." "Are you getting health and insurance benefits there?" "Uh, I don't think so." "And if they like you, like they did me, you could even move up the ladder yourself." "Let's not get ahead of ourselves." "I can't promise anything, but I'll interview for the job, and we'll take it from there. Deal?" "Deal."

We shake hands, and I go back to work. One lesson I've learned in life is that there are no coincidences. Everything happens for a reason, good or bad, it's meant to be. Some people call this fate; my father calls these Godences (Godly coincidences), which come divinely from God. But since they come from God, they aren't coincidences because HE has a reason and a purpose for creating them. Like the businessman in New York whose alarm mysteriously didn't go off one morning and was late for work. It was the morning of 9/11. He was supposed to be working in the *World Trade Center* that morning and would have been killed with hundreds of others if his alarm had gone off. Things all happen for a reason.

I left the restaurant, went back to work, and forgot about it. A week later I got a call from Bob, and sure enough, an interview had been set up with the Agency's HR department. The woman at the agency was very friendly, and the interview went very well. She asked me if I was offered the job would I be willing to leave the law office, I said "yes." She thanked me and said, "we'll be touch." I prayed about it that night, still unsure what to do. A step up would be great, but I also felt some loyalty to the law firm. Sure enough, I got the call a few days later, and they offered me the job. Woo-hoo! I told them I would need to give my current employers two weeks' notice, out of respect and they said fine.

I dreaded quitting my job, but I believed that the Lord had led me to this point and that he was giving me a fantastic opportunity. So I decided to take it. The next day, I went into the head lawyer's office and told him I had been offered another job. He was completely unfazed, "Okay, Jeff, whatever you need to do." "I guess this is my two weeks' notice." "Sounds good." That was it, I left. Woo-hoo! I was moving up, folks! Thank you, Lord! The following two weeks seemed like an eternity. They brought in a new mail guy, I trained him for a week, and that was that; I was gone. No watch, no golden parachute. I did my last day and moved on. The following Monday, I was going to work for one of LA's top advertising agencies *Wells, Rich, Greene*.

Monday morning came, and I was super excited! I went from a law office with lawyers and a staff of ten to a big ad agency on two floors with over 60 ad executives, copywriters, art directors, and support staff. It was awesome! However, working with more staff meant more mail and more work. I didn't stop to think what the job might entail. There were a lot of other duties that Bob conveniently forgot to mention, like making coffee when it ran out. In an ad agency, when every minute is go-time, that coffee pot had to be refilled constantly and was almost a separate job on its own. But I was grateful to Bob for getting me the job. I asked if I could take him to lunch, but he declined.

I found out later that Bob was not doing me any favors. He just needed somebody to take the job so he could "move up the ladder." I later learned that he disliked me and was actually jealous of me for some reason. It came to a head one day when the woman running HR overheard him shit-talking about me with another employee and she came down on him like a sledgehammer. It was only then that I realized what a dick Bob was and that he had been backstabbing me from the get-go.

Although the new job paid more money and had health benefits, there was a lot more work and a lot more stress. Advertising is a cutthroat business, and I could see the amount of pressure everyone was under. One day, I was working, and I suddenly felt a sharp pain in my stomach. It was like someone had stabbed me in the gut with a knife, and I had to go to the emergency room. The doctors said that I had a panic attack and that my intestines were all knotted up because of the stress from work.

It was then, I realized how good I had it at the law firm. It was super easy and there was zero stress. Be careful what you wish for. The new job was much worse than I realized, and I quit soon after that. Once again, I was unemployed, but at least I wasn't completely stressed out anymore, and I certainly didn't need any more trips to the hospital. One thing I knew for sure, I still needed to find a new agent to start modeling and acting again.

Then I saw a Game Show on TV called *The Gong Show*.

Chapter 13

The Gong Show

Some of you may remember *The Gong Show*, created and produced by *Chuck Barris*, who served as host for the NBC show. *The Gong Show* was known for its absurdist humor and style, with the actual competition being secondary to the often outlandish acts.

Celebrity judges, *Rip Tayler, Phyllis Diller* and *Chuck Woolery*

Each show presented a competition of amateur performers of often dubious talent, with a panel of three celebrity judges. The original program's regular judges were *Jamie Farr, Jaye P. Morgan, Arte Johnson, Phyllis Diller, Pat McCormick, Wayland Flowers, Anson Williams, Steve Garvey,* and *Rex Reed*. Throughout the program's run other celebrities included *David Letterman, Steve Martin, Mort Sahl, Pat Paulsen, Allen Ludden,* and *Sandy Duncan*.

If any judge considered an act particularly bad, they could force it to stop by striking a large gong. Barris would then ask the judge(s) why they had gonged the act, usually receiving a facetious response. Any act that survived without being gonged was given a score by the three judges on a scale of 0 to 10, for a maximum possible score of 30. The contestant who achieved the highest combined score won the grand prize: a check for $516.32 and a "Golden Gong" trophy.

Gong Show creator *Chuck Barris* gets a laugh from *The Unknown Comic*

Some of the true talents that appeared on the show were actor *Kevin Peter Hall*, who later appeared as the original *Predator* and as Harry in *Harry and the Hendersons*; and actor *Paul Reubens* (best known as *Pee Wee Herman*), impressionist and comedian, *Michael Winslow*; and an unknown band called *The Mystic Knights of the Oingo Boingo* which evolved into *Oingo Boingo*, led by future Oscar-winning composer *Danny Elfman*.

Murray Langston, The Unknown Comic who's act was to put a paper bag over his head and tell silly one-liner jokes would become a famous comedian playing in Las Vegas and around the world.

In 2017, a more recent version was created and executive-produced by *Will Arnett* and hosted by *Tommy Maitland*, a fictional character performed by actor and comedian *Mike Myers* (who was uncredited in Season 1). When Barris announced the final score, little person actor *Jerry Maren* (a former Munchkin from the *Wizard of Oz*) ran onstage in top hat and tails, throwing confetti while balloons dropped from overhead. Celebrity judges included *Megan Fox* and *Maya Rudolph*.

At the time, my twin brother Jerry and I were getting a lot of work, but we were always hungry for more. We watched the *Gong Show* and thought it was hilarious. We found out from some friends who were producers on the show that anyone could go in and audition, which we did. We didn't do it for the $516.32, but the nationwide exposure as *The Gong Show* was a hit TV show at the time. We would each cook up some ridiculous character and go in and audition separately. I don't know why we didn't go in as twins; we would have probably stood a better chance.

One day, Jerry goes in looking like a nerd, with pants that are too short, a wild patterned jacket, geeky glasses, greased-back hair, and an outlandish patterned tie. His schtick was to run up to the judge's table, shove his tie in their faces, and exclaim, "Hey! Do you like my tie? I got a new tie! He would then go down the row of judges and repeat the same lines, "Hey! Do you like my tie? I got a new tie! It was ridiculous and didn't show off any talent, but that's exactly what *The Gong Show* was all about. It was also absolutely hilarious. So they put Jerry on the show. Of course, it didn't take long for one of the judges to gong him (I think it was *J. P. Morgan*), but that made it all the more hilarious. Jerry was elated and couldn't wait to tell everyone that he was on *The Gong Show*. Unfortunately for me, none of my characters were able to pass the audition process and get on the show. Oh well, that's Hollywood. Yet my connection with the show and *Chuck Barris* would take an interesting but tragic turn.

About a year later, I was on the world-famous *Sunset Strip*. I had just come out of a local club and popped into a nearby liquor store, *Sunset Strip Liquor* that had been there for over sixty-five years. It was the go-to liquor store for the local residents or for anyone wanting to get some booze before or after one of the Rock n'

Roll shows taking place at any of the local clubs, like *The Whiskey A-Go-Go*, *The Roxy Theatre*, or *The Rainbow Room*. Legendary musicians and singers, including *Jim Morrison, Jimi Hendrix, The*

Sunset Strip Liquor - **Located on the *Sunset Strip* for over 65 years**

Rolling Stones, and you name it, all bought booze there at one time or another.

But at 1:00 am, I wasn't thinking about all the celebrities that had been there before; I just wanted a bottle of water as I was dehydrated from drinking at the club. So I'm inside the liquor store, and I see this beautiful blonde girl standing in front of the refrigerator that held all the beer. She has her face in her hands and was sobbing uncontrollably. I looked around and saw no one else in the store except us. I went over to her and asked, "Hey, are you okay?" she shook her head no. I said, "Did someone hurt you? Do you want me to get some help?" she shook her head again. She was a complete mess. I put a reassuring hand on her shoulder and said, "Tell me what happened."

After a moment, she said, "My boyfriend just broke up with me." And started to sob some more. I said, "Hey, forget about it, that's his loss; he doesn't know a good thing when he has it!" She stops crying, looks me in the eyes, and says, "You're very kind. You seem like a nice guy. I don't want to be alone right now. Do you want to get some beer and go back to my place? I live around the corner." I say, "Sure!" I bought some beer and walked her back to her apartment. It was a beautiful summer night in LA, and very romantic. I tell some jokes, she laughs, and we have instant chemistry. Her complete demeanor changed now, and she's funny and talkative. We're having a great time. We got to her apartment, which was literally right around the corner. She probably had some money because it was a lovely, upscale apartment, and anything near *The Sunset Strip* was quite expensive.

Della Barris

We walked in the door, and the first thing I saw was a huge framed photograph of Chuck Barris. I'm taken off-guard, laughed, and said, "What's Chuck Barris doing on your wall?" "Oh, That's my dad." What? I told her my Gong Show stories, and we laughed.

Pretty soon we were making out and the next thing you know, we're in her bed making love. Her name was *Della Barris*, Chuck's one and only child. Della was smart and sexy and had her dad's sense of humor and wit. It's not easy to find someone who could go toe-to-toe with me on the rector scale of comedy, but she did. I instantly started falling for her.

We were together for several months and things were going

great then I got busy with an acting job for a week. In order to make up for my absence I took her to a nice romantic dinner to discuss taking a vacation together. We laughed and caught up, but when I mentioned the vacation, she told me she had started seeing someone else and couldn't see me anymore. Seeing someone else? What are you talking about?

Della said she was extremely lonely and got depressed when she was alone. While I was busy working, she stayed home drinking and doing drugs with some new guy she met. Chuck payed all of her bills so she never had a job or ever had to work. I was devastated because I was falling in love with her. I shared my feelings and pleaded with her not to end our relationship but she wouldn't change her mind. It was then that I realized something was very wrong, but I honored her wishes and moved on.

Five years later I read that Della was found dead in her apartment from an overdose of drugs and alcohol at the age of 36. My heart sank when I heard the news that reported Della was HIV-positive, bipolar, an alcoholic and drug addict. I didn't know about her psychological issues, if I did, I would have tried to help her. When she said she was lonely and depressed, I didn't realize how deep-rooted her issues were.

If you or someone you know is struggling with depression, you can call or text these crisis hotlines: Call 988, or chat at 988lifeline.org

I'm grateful for the time Della and I had together. I know that I was meant to meet her in that liquor store on Sunset Blvd. at 1:00 am, if only to help her briefly through a sad time of pain and sorrow.

Chuck wrote a book to deal with her death titled Della: A Memoir of my Daughter where he describes her battle with drugs and alcohol and how with all his money and power, even he couldn't save her. Chuck passed away ten years later. He and Della were finally reunited. Heaven does exist and one day we will all be reunited with our lost loved ones.

Chapter 14

Back to the Mansion

The Mansion is 21,987 sq. ft. and sits on 5.3 acres of land

I had been back in LA for almost a year and I was so busy working that I didn't stop to think about reconnecting with *Playboy*. I once again called Playboy Corporate and found someone who connected me with the *Playboy Mansion*. Her name was Jenny. She was very sweet, and I told her that I had worked at *The Empire Club* in New York and that my brother and I had been invited to one of Hef's Sunday Screening Parties a few years earlier. She asked me to send over some photos (unless you're a personal friend, or major celebrity, Mansion party guests are selected personally by Hef through submitted photographs).

I sent her some of my head shots along with some newspaper articles and photos of me in *People Magazine* and of course Playboy.

She called and said that Hef would love to have me come as his guest to the upcoming *Mid-Summer Nights Dream Party* at the

Mansion. Just so you know, the Mid-Summer Night's Dream Party was one of the best Mansion parties all year, where everyone was either dressed in pajamas, boxer shorts or as in most cases for the women, sexy lingerie. The only party better than this one was Hef's extravagant Halloween Party.

Let me rewind a bit. When Jerry and I had gone to the Playboy Mansion for Hef's *Sunday Screening Night*, it was not my first time to the Mansion. It was the first time as a guest. Remember back in the day when I had to work as a waiter, bartender, etc. to support myself while pursuing acting? Well, I also worked for the Valet Parking company, parking cars for private parties and events. That was my first brush with real celebrities. I would work all the high-end parties in Beverly Hills, Bel-Air and the Hollywood Hills. The parties in the hills really blew, because we would have to run up and down the hills all night to park and retrieve the cars.

If you couldn't run in black dress shoes, a white buttoned down dress shirt, black bow-tie and standard Valet red vest (with a V logo on it), then you didn't park cars for Valet. I eventually worked my way up to supervisor, which meant I ran the show. I had a crew of 4-8 guys (depending on the size of the party). I handed out the parking claim tickets directly to the customers and was responsible for everything until the last car had left at the end of the night. Not only was I the man in charge, I didn't have to run anymore, my Team did. One night I was working a birthday party for *Joe Weider* (one of the top physical trainers and body builders in the world at the time).

Jack LaLanne, another famous trainer and body builder that had his own hit television show, drives up to the house. I send one of the guys to park his car. Jack was a great guy with a huge personality and talked with us for a few minutes before going into the party. He was about 70 years-old at the time and was still in fantastic shape.

Jack LaLanne: Do guys know I can still do one-armed push-ups?

Me: Really, let's see!

Jack LaLanne: Watch this fellas...

117

He takes his jacket off, gets down on the ground and starts doing one-armed push-ups.

Me: Wow, you're in great shape!

Jack LaLanne: It's all part of a healthy diet, and daily workout regime.

We thought we were watching a commercial for Jack LaLanne fitness. He sounded just like he did on TV, the perfect pitchman. He turns to me.

Jack LaLanne: Tell you what, I'll give you a hundred bucks right now if you can do 100 regular push-ups!

Me: Okay! I take off my jacket and get down on the ground.

I started doing regular push-ups and got to about 53 when I ran out of steam and collapsed. I got up off the ground and Jack slapped me on the back.

Jack LaLanne: That's okay kid, keep working on it.

He put his jacket back on and went into the party. My crew gave me a hard time after that for failing to win the $100 prize. A short time later, a big Mercedes Benz pulled up. I opened the door for the driver and *Arnold Schwarzenegger* got out.

I handed him a parking claim ticket and he started giving me driving instructions. You have to understand that by now, I've driven and parked everything from a Volkswagen to a Lamborghini.

Me: Good evening Mr. Schwarzenegger....

Arnold Schwarzenegger: Zis is zee parking brake and zis is zee release

Me: Yes sir, I know...

Arnold Schwarzenegger: Please be careful...zis is my baby!

Me: Yes sir, of course sir.

Arnold handed me the keys and went inside the party. As soon as he was inside, I jumped into his car and floored it. The tires squealed as I drove it up the street as fast as I could and parked it, just so I could say that I drove Arnold Schwarzenegger's car.

We did a lot of crazy stuff, but I never damaged anyone's car or got in an accident. A lot of other guys did, however. Another perk to parking cars at the A-List parties was a lot of beautiful women would arrive. I would open their door, welcome them and give them a parking stub. Since I was now the supervisor, I wore an actual sport coat and straight tie, so I looked pretty sharp (instead of the red vest and bow tie that runners wore which made them look like waiters).

Sometimes the women would come out of the party and start chatting me up complaining that the party was boring. Sometimes they would even bring me drinks and since I wasn't parking anyone's car, I went for it. One time, one of the drunken ladies actually performed oral sex on me in her parked car, at the party. Like I said, we did some crazy stuff. I received nothing but great reviews from the party hosts and was soon getting booked on all the top echelon parties and events. One day, one of the managers called me at 11:00am in the morning on my day off.

Valet Manager: Hey Jeff, I just had one of my guys cancel on me for a luncheon at 12:00 noon. I know it's last minute notice but can you help me out?

Me: Sure.

Valet Manager: I appreciate it. This is a great job and if you do good, I'll take care of you.

Me: No Problem. Where am I going?

Valet Manager: The Playboy Mansion.

Me: Really?

Valet Manager: Yeah, one of my regular guys called in sick. If you do good, I'll give you his regular spot.

Me: You can count on me.

Valet Manager: Good. A few things, Mr. Hefner expects complete professionalism. There were some complaints about one of the guys getting too friendly with the Playmates.

Me: I understand sir, you don't have to worry about me.

Valet Manager: Good, because that employee is no longer working for the company.

Me: I understand. Thank you for this opportunity, I won't let you down.

Valet Manager: I know you won't.

From that day forward I was a regular Valet at the Playboy Mansion during Hef's regular lunchtime events. One particular day, a Playmate drove up in her convertible sports car. I opened the door and greeted her. She swung her legs out of the car.

Playmate: Oops, I forgot to put on my panties....

She did indeed not have any underwear on and she made sure I saw it. She looked at me and smiled.

Playmate: You won't tell on me will you?

Me: No Ma'am, it'll be our little secret.

Playmate: You're so sweet.

Me: Enjoy your lunch ma'am.

She smiled and went inside. There were several occasions when women would flirt with me, but I was always professional. I wasn't going to jeopardize this gig for a one night stand. I was smart, because soon, I would be moving to the big show. The mansion's night-time parties, where only the very top Valet guys were lucky enough to work.

It was the annual *Mid-Summer Nights Dream Party* and all the women were arriving in sexy and incredibly skimpy lingerie. Me and the other Valet guys always kidded about crashing one of the parties some night when we weren't working. But of course, we never did. We had a good thing going and we weren't about to screw it up. But I told the guys in no uncertain terms, "One day I'm going to be inside the Mansion partying, but it's because I'll be somebody and I'll be invited, not because I crashed it. Little did I know that years later, that would be just one of my self-fulfilling prophecies.

Okay, flash forward to real time. Jenny said that I would receive an invitation in the mail, but I would still need to call and RSVP. Call right away she said, as the RSVP list fills up rather quickly. I'll bet. I got the invitation and RSVP'd right away. Only Hef's closest friends and special guests get to actually drive their cars to the Mansion. Everyone else is driven up in 40-person passenger Shuttle Vans from a UCLA parking structure where everyone parks and is checked in. I parked in the structure and went over to the check-in table where I met Jenny for the first time. She was a very attractive brunette in her 30's. I thanked her for getting me on the guest list and was given a wrist-band. I boarded the Shuttle Van along with 39 other VIP guests which were mostly women (either Playmates, actresses or supermodels), they were all stunning!

We arrived at the Mansion which had buku security as you might imagine. As we got off the shuttle, our wristbands were once again checked by security and we made our way towards the front door. There was a team of about ten Valet Parking Attendants, all at attention waiting to park the VIP cars that were arriving. I walked right up to one of the Valet guys, and looked him right in the eye.

> Me: I used to be you.
> Valet Attendant: Huh?
> Me: Yeah, I used to work for Valet and park cars up here too.
> Valet Attendant: Really?

Me: That's right. And I told myself that one day, I would be successful enough in Hollywood to be invited to the The Playboy Mansion as a guest, not as a Valet.

> I took a beat as he took in all this information.
> Me: And today, is that day my friend.
> Valet Attendant: Wow!

Me: (I pointed right at him) And you can too! You can do and be anything you want in this world...don't let anyone tell you, you can't!

> Valet Attendant: Yeah. (getting pumped up)

All of a sudden his face lit up and his demeanor instantly changed. I could see that he had a new found sense of inspiration and excitement.

> Me: Remember what I told you here tonight.
> Valet Attendant: I will. Thank you sir!
> Me: Don't mention it.

And with that, I strolled into my first major party at the Playboy Mansion and the adventure that lay ahead.

Upon entering the Mansion, I was greeted by several more people and even more security. I took it all in, it was like Disneyland for adults, amazing. There had to be 700-800 guests in lingerie, boxer shorts and assorted undergarments. There were usually five different food stations with an assortment of gourmet cuisine. A sushi bar, a seafood bar (with shrimp, crab legs, oysters and lobster), a salad bar, a dessert bar and the grand buffet with succulent prime

The Foyer and Grand Staircase of the Mansion

rib and an assortment of side dishes. There were three main bars, one in the front, one in the middle and one in the back by the famous Grotto. Each bar had three to four bartenders in order to keep the drinks flowing. This was one party you never had to wait more than a couple of a minutes to get a drink and with all the celebrities and eye-candy everywhere, there was plenty to look at while you were waiting.

I had a regular routine every time I went to the Mansion, (probably about thirty times over the years). Since I knew I would be drinking (along with everyone else) all night long, I always started by having dinner. I'd start with the seafood buffet, with the Shrimp, crab legs, lobster and some sushi. I've never cared for raw oysters and I certainly didn't need help getting sexually motivated at the Playboy Mansion.

After the seafood appetizer I'd make my way to the buffet for some meat and potatoes, salad, etc. I saved the dessert bar for later in the evening when I needed a sugar rush. It turned out that one of my friends from High School (William Howard Taft) was the pastry chef at the mansion. We played a little catch up and I told her that I had worked for Playboy in New York. Small world.

I put my plate of food down on one of the nearby tables and sat down. As I looked up, famed comedian and actor *Red Buttons* was sitting right across the table from me. I said, "Hello Red, I love your work!" He smiled and said thank you. He had to have been at least 80 years old, but he still looked great and still had a twinkle in his eye. Part of his famous comedy routine, was that he would say that he had been at some big fancy awards show and was the only person who "didn't get a dinner." Well at the Playboy Mansion, I guarantee you *Red Buttons* got a dinner!

I finished eating and decided it was time to have a cocktail and get in the groove. My drink of choice was usually a Silver Patron Margarita on the rocks with no salt, a lime and a splash of orange juice. I got my first margarita of the night and started my stroll through the revelry. The coolest thing about the mansion was, once you're inside, everybody was treated the same no matter who you were. Everyone knew that when you're at that party, you're somebody special, or you wouldn't be there. I'm headed toward the other side of the room and I run into comedic actor *Jack Black (Tenacious D)*, so I introduced myself.

Me: Hey Jack, I'm Jeff Rector...
Jack Black: Hey man! How's it going?
Me: Pretty good, nice to meet you.
Jack Black: Nice to meet you too.

He was just like most of the characters he plays in the movies, he had a big smile, a lot of energy and a really cool vibe. I continued on and saw *David Hasselhoff* talking to a couple of ladies. He was wearing pajama bottoms, a bathrobe and a t-shirt that said, "Don't Hassle The Hoff!" Other mansion regulars included *Bill Maher* and *Kato Kaelin*. I ran into a couple of friends and we joked around for a few minutes until it was time to freshen up our cocktails. I

went up to a different bar and was waiting to get the bartenders attention and standing next to me was actress *Michelle Rodriguez* who stars in the *Fast and Furious* movies. Not all stars look as good in person as they do on the screen, but she did. She was stunning. I said hello, she smiled and said hi. She got her drink and took off. I got another margarita and continued the circuit, briefly talking to *Ben Affleck* and a few other very recognizable

Jeff and *David Hasselhoff*

celebrities.

World famous body builder and actor *Lou Ferrigno (The Incredible Hulk)* and his beautiful wife Carla were regulars there, and I would see them on many occasions. I started a website design business a few years later and actually redesigned Lou's website for him. Lou was probably one of the nicest and most sincere people you could ever meet. Later on in the evening, my friend Tom came up to me all excited.

Tom: "You'll never guess who just walked in?"

I'm thinking Angelina Jolie, Jennifer Aniston or Denise Richards.

Me: (Excited) "Who is it?

Tom: (He could barely contain himself) "It's Amy from "The Apprentice!"

Me: Amy from The Apprentice? Donald Trump's reality show? Didn't she just get fired?

Tom: Yeah, but she just walked in!

It was at that moment that I realized how impactful reality shows were going to be, and how nobodies could instantly become celebrities just because they're on TV. It was also to the point where every new reality show that got green-lit, a scripted drama or sitcom did not. Which meant there was less acting work for me and everybody else. When I talked to my agent about it and expressed my concern, he said "Don't worry about it Jeff, Reality Shows are only a fad!"

Well we know that wasn't the case, because today, about 60% of television programming is some form of reality show. Well, Tom went over to talk to her, and I went back to the bar for another drink. I saw *James Franco* at the bar talking to a pretty blonde. I had met him several times before, and so I walked over to say hi. He recognized me, said hello, and introduced me to his blonde friend.

James Franco: Jeff, do you know *Paris Hilton*? (I suddenly recognized her).
Me: No, I don't. Nice to meet you Paris.
Paris Hilton: Nice to meet you too Jeff.

I got another drink and we all chatted it up for awhile. I found Paris to be quite nice and charming and James Franco was a really cool, down to earth guy. Not wanting to be rude, I told James it was good to see him, I told Paris it was nice meeting her, and I was on my way.

When I first started going to the mansion, photographs were strictly forbidden. Hef didn't want unauthorized pictures of his playmates and his celebrity friends to find their way into newspapers and magazines, and neither did they. Security would confiscate any cameras that they saw and would hold them until that person left at the end of the night. A lot of times if you disobeyed the "house rules" and were caught with a camera, you might not be invited back again. Although security seemed to be a little more flexible with the ladies, than the guys.

I was getting a pretty good buzz on about now and found myself on the dance floor with a couple of Playmates. Hef always had one of the top DJ's playing great dance music and sometimes there would be a live band as well, especially for the New Year's Eve party. We were all dancing and having a great time. I looked and saw Hef finally coming to the party. He would usually show up around 10:00pm or so, accompanied by his gorgeous girlfriends and a team of security. He would have his own private area to mingle with certain special party guests.

I left the dance floor and headed over to the bar by the heated swimming pool, waterfall and the famous *Grotto*. There was a big bar by the swimming pool, it was a favorite hang-out because it was close to the outside patio, and the co-ed restrooms where people would congregate as well. There were two bartenders there that were identical twins. They were really nice guys and we had some laughs when I told them that I was an identical twin as well. They made me a margarita (big surprise) and I decided it was time to take a peek in *The Grotto*.

The Grotto

The Grotto was a man-made cave that was part of the landscaping of the mansions enormous swimming pool. There was an enormous rock formation with a waterfall that the pool surrounds and led directly into *The Grotto*. So you could walk into it from the bar side, or literally swim into it from the pool side through

the waterfall. Inside *The Grotto* were several large in-ground Jacuzzi's that could fit 15-20 people comfortably or 30-40 people very comfortably! Surrounding the jacuzzi's were areas that people could sit and talk or remove their clothes and get into the swirling hot water. Because the jacuzzi's were in a cave, the hot water heated the air inside, so it was like a sauna. You couldn't stay in there too long, it was just too hot. But if you swam from *The Grotto* out into the swimming pool, it was cooler and felt fantastic.

The swimming pool surrounds the waterfall leading into *The Grotto*

Since people were usually naked in *The Grotto*, it was natural that sex was going to happen. Any stories you've heard bout *The Grotto* are probably true. One particular party, I ran into an old girlfriend of mine out of the blue who was there with her girlfriend. They were pretty wasted and asked if I wanted to go into *The Grotto* with them. Let me think...YES! We all got naked and descended into the steaming water, it was fairly early in the evening and there weren't a lot of people inside yet. The next thing I know, I'm sandwiched in between them and the rest is history. We dried off, got dressed and I went out on the patio for a cigarette. I wasn't really smoking at the time, but it seemed like the natural thing to do.

The grounds of the mansion were amazing! There were several separate large guesthouses, each with four or five "private bedrooms" where guests could get busy if they so chose. One of the guesthouses had a "Game Room" with a pool table, several pinball machines and assorted video games. The grounds were tiered with several different levels and various gardens that guests could wander around and disappear for romantic interludes. There was also a small zoo on the back part of the property with monkey cages and assorted wild life. The monkeys would come right up to the front of the cage and reach their little fingers through so you could touch them. One couple was smoking a joint and they blew the smoke into the monkey's face. I think they got him stoned, because about fifteen minutes later, he was jumping around inside the cage having the time of his life. A short distance from the monkey cages were several animals including a beautiful peacock. Behind the zoo were steps leading down to another level of the grounds with pathways leading to different areas that had benches to sit and relax and take in the surroundings.

One particular bench was my favorite and was right in the middle of a group of huge trees and foliage. If you didn't know you were on the Mansion grounds, you'd think you were in the middle of a rain forest somewhere in the Congo. It was extremely private, and I'll bet that most guests to the Mansion had never even been there before or knew about it. I wouldn't have found it, except my second or third trip I decided to do some exploring and wandered down one of the trails and stumbled upon it. It was my favorite place, because it was private and on more than one occasion, I had sensual encounters with several female guests.

Jeff in his blue silk pajamas

There was a special indescribable magic at the Playboy Mansion, where your inhibitions were discarded and an air of sexual freedom was prevalent. Everyone, especially the ladies were barely wearing any clothes (scanty lingerie) and some women were completely nude with an assortment of artful body painting. The men, as I mentioned, were in boxer shorts, bathrobes, t-shirts, flannel pajamas, etc. In honor of Hef's usual silk pajamas and famous smoking jacket, I usually wore my pair of navy blue silk pajamas that I got in Hong Kong when I worked with Jean-Claude Van Damme on the film Double Impact. I also picked up a red, short, silk, patterned bathrobe as well. Sometimes I would wear the silk pajamas, other times I would wear the pajama bottoms and the silk bathrobe without the pajama top. The pajamas are still sitting in my closet as a reminder of the crazier days in my life. The only time I ever wore those silk pajamas was to the Playboy Mansion.

The Mid-Summer Night's Dream Party was one of the best party's, because it usually took place in August, one of the hottest months of the year in Los Angeles. The party was both indoors and outdoors, under the beautiful night sky filled with a glowing, radiant moon and peaceful bright stars. It was almost as if the moon was looking down on us, saying to itself, "You lucky bastards!"

For Halloween, because in October the weather was much colder, huge white tents would be erected to cover the pool area all the way up to the Mansions back patio. When the whole area was enclosed within the tents, you didn't even realize that you were actually outside the main house. If you had never been outside on the grounds in the summer, you wouldn't even know that you were actually in the back yard, because the tents were so tall, you just assumed that was the roof. The illusion was further enhanced with carpeting laid down on the patio floor. The illusion that you were still inside The Playboy Mansion was quite simply amazing.

Hef's Horror Halloween Party

As amazing as the Mid-Summer Night's Dream party was, nothing could top Hef's annual Halloween extravaganza. For this Party, (usually the Saturday before Halloween), Hef brought in a team of Hollywood's top decorators, prop masters, make-up artists and special effects wizards, turning the Playboy Mansion into a Halloween House of Horror. Actors were hired to play an assortment of monsters, ghouls, and zombies that would be placed and hidden throughout the grounds to surprise and scare unsuspecting guests. No place at the mansion was safe.

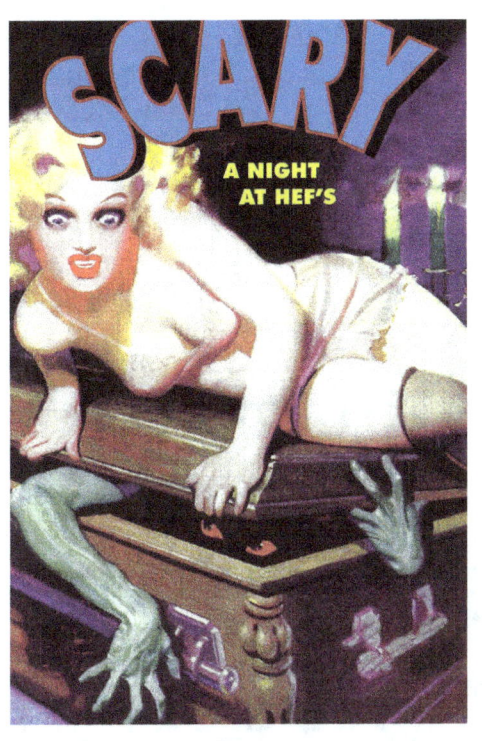

Here's my experience; 'I'd park my car at the UCLA Parking Structure, (which was later changed to a Century City location). I'd check in with Jenny or Mary, get my wristband and get on the shuttle bus. As we drove up the long driveway to the mansion, about halfway up, we suddenly stopped. We began wondering if there was a problem with the engine. Suddenly, out of the bushes, a horde of flesh-eating zombies attacked the bus pounding on the glass, and trying to get in to eat our brains. Most of the guys laughed, but the majority of the women on the bus screamed at the top their lungs they were so scared. The bus started moving again and the zombies continued to pound on the windows and the side of the bus until we were a safe distance away.

The bus continued up the hill to the point where you saw the mansion as it first came into view. This was an eerie throwback to my first experience seeing the mansion for the very first time. This time though, as we pulled up to the central fountain and circular driveway, it was an all together different scenario. Looming above part of the mansion was an enormous animatronic demon with glowing red eyes and flapping wings that had to have a wingspan of at least 60 feet. We'd get off the bus to see that the entire (huge) front yard was dressed as an elaborate cemetery, complete with tombstones, stone gargoyles and even a mausoleum or two. The cemetery was lit with studio mood lighting to give it an eerie, surreal look and feel, complete with a bank of fog running through it (courtesy of special effects fog machines).

Inside the Haunted Playboy Mansion, each room was decorated with a different theme. One room was dressed as a funeral parlor with a corpse laying in the casket on display. As soon as anyone got close enough to look at the decaying corpse, it sprang to life scaring the bejeezus out of them. Another room had a series of really cool monster heads (some of them decapitated), with props from famous horror films on display. For the Halloween party, instead of pajamas and lingerie, everyone wore costumes. Actresses, models

and Playmates were dressed as everything from topless Catholic schoolgirls to one Playmate dressed as Lady Godiva, (who was literally naked because she could). Only at the Playboy Mansion. So in addition to the most expensive cast and crew and Halloween decorations in the world (probably over $100,000), everyone was running around in super-sexy costumes or nothing at all.

The coolest thing at the party, was that one of the back guesthouses was turned into an interactive walk-through Haunted House, with elaborate set-dressing, monsters, live actors, and motion picture-grade animatronics. One room recreated a scene from *William Friedkin's* classic supernatural horror film *The Exorcist*. The film starred an unknown young actress named *Linda Blair,* whose harrowing performance still haunts viewers today. Linda, was so good in the role, that it made her an instant overnight movie star. The downside was, that for many years she would only be offered roles predominantly in the supernatural horror genre. I got to know Linda over the years, having done a lot of autograph signing events with her. She is one of the sweetest and kindest people I know, (the exact opposite of the demonic monster she portrayed on screen). She is also an animal rights activist and has her own ongoing charity for animals donating the money she makes from personal appearances to support animals in need.

To get to the Haunted House, you had to take the walkway alongside the cemetery. Spooky sounds filled the air (from hidden speakers throughout the area). As you come down the walkway, an occasional werewolf, zombie or demon would jump out at you. Because the Haunted Guest House was always the hit of the party, there was probably a forty-five minute to an hour wait to get inside. The good news was, you had plenty of time to chat up the models and playmates that were also waiting in line. This was cool, because when we finally went in together every time they got scared, they'd grab onto me for safety. On more than one occasion, this "bonding" led to more personal adult interaction once we got outside of the haunted house.

Hef's Halloween Party was also cool because a lot of famous actresses and supermodels would wear heavy make-up cover-

James Bond with Elvira, Wonder Woman and a Bunny on Halloween

ing their identities so that they could take-a-walk-on-the-wild-side without anyone knowing who they were. I know this, because I was with one such actress (that will remain nameless) that confided in me after we took a walk past the monkey cages to my "secret place." Halloween has always been my favorite holiday because everyone can be or wear whatever they want. I'm always surprised by the level of creativity, especially when people make their own costumes.

I've been a long time sci-fi, horror geek, and this party was the monster of all Halloween parties. I went to these parties (and others) at the mansion for another ten years or so, until Jenny's departure from Playboy. They decided to downsize and reduce the number of guests. When Jenny left, so did anyone on her guest list which included a hundred or so semi-regulars like myself.

In January 2016, the Playboy Mansion was put on the market for $200 million, with the condition that *Hugh Hefner* would continue to work and live in the mansion. Later that year it was sold for $100 million.

On September 27th, 2017 *Hugh Hefner* died at the mansion in Holmby Hills at the age of 91. The cause was sepsis brought on by an E. coli infection. He is interred at *Westwood Memorial Park* in Los Angeles, in a $75,000 crypt beside *Marilyn Monroe*. "Spending eternity next to Marilyn was an opportunity too sweet to pass up," Hefner had told the Los Angeles Times in 2009.

I will always be grateful to *Hugh Hefner, Christie Hefner,* and Jenny for including me in their elite group of friends and participating in a once-in-a-lifetime adventure that will never be seen or experienced ever again.

Up until now I enjoyed some success in Hollywood doing some stand-in work for *Charlie Sheen, Tom Cruise* and *Kevin Spacey.* What I didn't know was that my next job was right around the corner and would involve working with *Richard Gere, Julia Roberts,* and *Garry Marshall* on the box-office hit *Pretty Woman.*

Chapter 15

Pretty Woman

As I recall, my brother Jerry got a call from *Central Casting* saying that director *Garry Marshall* was looking for a stand-in

and photo double for *Richard Gere* for his next film, *Three Thousand*. The name was derived from the amount (three thousand dollars) that Richard Gere's character pays *Julia Roberts'* hooker character to spend the weekend with him in Beverly Hills.

Although I was slightly shorter than Richard, who is six feet tall, to my five feet ten inches, I had plenty of stand-in work with major stars, which seemed more important to Garry and Richard. An actor has to work with their stand-in all day, every day, for the entire production run (usually about three months for a major film with a large budget). Garry liked the fact that Jerry and I were twins, and we could serve double duty since they needed both a stand-in and a photo double for Richard. This also worked in our favor when we doubled for *Jean-Claude Van Damme* on *Double Impact*.

Garry wanted to hire us both for the stand-in and photo double roles since they could both be shot simultaneously using two different film crews, which would save production time and money. Since Jerry was the first contact, they gave him the choice of jobs. He chose the body doubling, thinking that it would be the best of both gigs, especially when he found out that Richard would be driving a Lamborghini around in the film and that Jerry would be the guy driving the car most of the time.

As production began, Jerry started by doubling Richard in most of the driving sequences at the beginning of the film. Richard gets lost in the Hollywood Hills and winds up on Hollywood Blvd., where he meets Julia Roberts. At the same time, I would begin filming with the main production crew as Richard's stand-in. As it turned out, I ended up with a better job since I had worked for three months on the film. They initially promised Jerry more work in the beginning but used him a lot less than he had anticipated.

On my first day working with Richard, the production put me in an identical suit he wore in the film and a salt-and-pepper wig that matched his hairstyle. We were standing next to each other on Hollywood Blvd. We had already met a few minutes earlier when I was officially introduced to him. He smiled his rakish Gere grin and said nice to meet you, and we shook hands. As I mentioned earlier, when an actor is a stand-in for a major star or any actor really, the rule of thumb is to keep your eyes open and your mouth shut. You only talk to the stars if they talk to you. Richard looks over at me in my matching suit and wig and says, "Not bad for a dime-store wig," I say, "Yeah, it's not bad."

Richard has always been a fantastic actor, and I remember seeing him for the first time in *American Gigolo*. I thought, wow, who is that guy, he's terrific. Richard would star in films like *An Officer and a Gentleman, Primal Fear, Unfaithful,* and *First Knight* with Sean Connery. But none of his movies would be more popular or successful than Pretty Woman, which has grossed over $463.4 million dollars to date. The first time you see the film (or the twentieth time), the chemistry between Richard and Julia is undeniable and magnetic. Everyone on set could see a natural, true attraction that went way beyond the script.

As his stand-in, I was working every day with Richard and became officially part of the cast and crew, and whenever they needed a photo double, they just used me as opposed to hiring Jerry for one day here and there since I was already on the set and available. I also got to drive the Lamborghini, except for the opening scene. It was me driving the car throughout the rest of the film, and when you saw Richard's hand shifting the gears on the Lanbourgini, it was actually an insert of my hand doing the shifting.

I found out later that Garry Marshall had a natural affinity for twins; if you look back on many of his films, you'll see cameos with identical twins. Garry was great to work with and was one of the nicest directors I've ever had the pleasure of working with. About two-thirds through the production, there was a swimming pool scene we shot at the *Ambassador Hotel* (where *Robert Kennedy* was assassinated). In its heyday in the 40's and 50's, the Ambassador Hotel was one of the most prestigious hotels in Los Angeles for celebrities and tourists who could afford to stay there. The hotel had been closed for many years and was used primarily for filming purposes.

Garry liked my brother and I and put us in the scene at the pool as twin lifeguards. Although we didn't have any dialogue, we would be featured in a major film for *Touchstone Pictures*, which was owned by *Disney*. The scene entailed *Julia Roberts* walking around the pool to meet someone. They were very long takes since she had to walk around a huge pool to get to her final mark (filming position).

There was a lot of dead time with no dialogue as she walked. I decided to take a chance and, during one take (since I was a lifeguard), yelled out to one of the kids in the pool, "Hey you, stop splashing... I'm going to remember your face!" At the end of the take, Garry yelled, "Cut!" Nobody said anything to me, so I kept saying the same line during each additional take. After about the third or fourth take, the assistant director approached me and said, you have your SAG card, right? I said yes. He said, "Good, Garry likes what you're doing, so keep doing it. I'll give you a contract at the end of the day".

Woo-hoo! I took a chance, and it paid off! We did the scene a couple of more times and moved on. Sure enough, at the end of the day, I was given a SAG Principal contract, which not only meant I would have a speaking role in the film, but my day rate went from $125 a day to over $600 for the day. The pool scene started with *Julia Roberts* walking around the pool; then I said my lines, and then the camera came around and ended with Jerry talking to a cute girl in a bikini. Even though he didn't have any lines, we both were in the scene as identical pool lifeguards.

I found out a week later that the producers didn't like the pool's look since it didn't look as glamorous on screen as they would have liked, so they decided to reshoot the entire pool sequence. All that hard work is down the drain. A week later, I was notified that we would be re-shooting the pool scene in Westwood in one of the newer, sexier, more modern hotel pools. This time, because the pool was much smaller, I would not be a lifeguard but a pool attendant. Jerry wasn't scheduled to shoot; only a few extras were needed instead of the thirty or so used in the previous shoot.

When I got to the set, Garry asked me if I wanted to be in the scene, and I said absolutely! They re-wrote the scene with Julia meeting actress and co-star *Laura San Giacomo* for an intimate lunch poolside. As Julia arrives, she approaches me and says, "Hey Mitchell, where would you like me to sit?" I reply, "Anywhere you like." We get the scene in about three takes. The scene then moves to a lunch table where Julia is talking to Laura. I come to the table to take their lunch order, and Julia says, "I'll have the Cobb salad." I then turn to Laura and say, "And?" she says, "The same," and then I reply, "I'll be right back."

Wow, I went from throwing out a generic line to someone in the pool to having a scene with *Julia Roberts* and me and then a second scene with Julia and Laura. I was so grateful to Garry for such a fantastic opportunity. He could have easily not put me in the scene once they did the re-shoot—yet another perk of being the stand-in. I was already there on the set working for Richard, so it was much easier to be added to the scene without them having to cast someone else in the part. Once again, we got it in two or three takes. I was ecstatic! I went to work in the morning as a stand-in and came home a principal actor in a Garry Marshall film that millions of people would see.

I didn't tell Jerry right away because he was already upset that I got to work so many more days than he did, but as I said, he was the one who chose his role in the first place. But that happens to everyone. We've all made decisions that we later regretted in our careers or lives. Knowing what I knew from all the stand-in work I've done, I would not have made the same choice. The irony would hit me when I was personally invited to the star-studded cast and crew Red Carpet Premier in Hollywood. As bad luck would have it, the pool scenes I shot were entirely cut from the film—all those days of filming, locations, crew, etc. No Julia, No Laura and no Jeff.

I wasn't the only person who wound up on the cutting room floor. Many other stand-ins and even some principal actors that were cast in the film, including Garry's daughter, got cut too. The original version ran too long, so the editor needed to trim the film to keep it moving. It was the obvious choice, and the success of the final version proved it. Although many of us were cut from the final version, according to the SAG contact, we had to get paid and still receive residual checks even though we weren't ever seen in the final version. Thank you, SAG! Even to this day, I still get checks once in a while from "Pretty Woman."

About a month into the production, I heard that Garry was looking for a body double for *Julia Roberts* for some of the semi-nude shots as well as some insert shots of Julia getting dressed as the prostitute (putting on the now-famous black vinyl high-heeled boots, jewelry, etc.). At the time, my girlfriend was a beautiful

Jeff, Shelley and *Joe Mantegna*

actress, model, singer, and dancer named *Shelley Michelle* (her stage name). Her real name was *Shelley Michelle Winnaman*. She was tall and statuesque, with long, beautiful legs and a perfectly proportioned body.

Shelley Michelle

We had just gotten back from *Big Bear*, where her parents had a house on the lake. We took their boat out waterskiing, and I took a great shot of her standing on the boat's bow in her bikini, wearing a captain's cap. She perfectly matched Julia's long, shapely legs and body. I took the picture and showed it to Garry. He immediately called her in for an interview, and that was it; she was hired as Julia's body double. Unfotunately I was working long hours five days a week. But when we both worked on set we had time to see each other, get paid and have some fun.

Jeff and *Donna Scoggins* (photo doubles)

They even used me to double Richard on the now famous *Pretty Woman* poster, where he and Julia are back to back, and she's tugging on his suit tie. We got a lot of additional publicity from all the gossip magazines because of how popular the movie was. Shelley then took it to the next level and contacted various magazines and news outlets to gain additional media exposure. She would call me and say, "Hey, what are you doing tomorrow? I have another interview with this magazine or news show."

At one point, because she was over-publicizing that she was body doubling for Julia, the studio told her she couldn't talk about it anymore because it was reducing the magic and romanticism of the love story between her and Richard.

I have to credit Shelley; I've never seen anyone take an opportunity like that and milk it the way she she did. Today, she is still considered the world's most famous body double. She even opened her own modeling agency called *Body Doubles and Parts*. Years later, I would still get calls from Shelley saying that she had an interview with some European magazine and that I would be interested in being part of it. By this time, I was a working actor, and I'd say, "Shelley, please stop telling people that I'm a body double; I don't do that anymore!" I must say, though, that Shelley took that opportunity and turned it into a lifetime of marketing and promotion.

One day, I'm on the set, the cameras and lights are all set up, but nothing was happening. I ask one of the grips why everyone was just sitting around and why we weren't shooting. The grip said we've been waiting for Richard and Julia for an hour and a half. I said, where are they? He said they were in Julia's trailer. A few minutes later, Richard nonchalantly emerged from her trailer, followed by Julia, who looked slightly embarrassed. Garry Marshall immediately yells, "Okay, Richard and Julia are here! They walk onto the set, take their places, and Garry yells, "Action!" We started to shoot again, and everything went back to normal.

The shoot, for the most part, went very smoothly. At the time, Julia Roberts was a relatively unknown actress; her biggest credit was a film called *Mystic Pizza*. Many name actresses were considered for the role (which were the studio's choices), but Garry pushed hard for her and cast Julia. As shooting went on, there was a lot of buzz on set that the movie would bomb. Even though Richard and Julia had great chemistry and were great together, the plot about a handsome, wealthy businessman who picks up a hooker (with a heart) on Hollywood Blvd. and then falls in love with her was just too implausible.

Production on the film was finally completed, and the cast and crew wrap party took place at *Pickwick Bowling Alley* in Burbank. There was food, drinks, and bowling. Garry Marshall and his son Scott both played drums, so a drum set and piano were brought in. Richard played the piano, Garry and Scott played the drums, and Julia sang. After a while, I jumped in and sang a few songs with Julia. It was a fantastic way to finish what had become an incredible three-month experience for me. Now, all that was left was for the film to be edited and to go through the post-production process, about another three to four months.

Garry changed the title from *Three Thousand* to *Pretty Woman* and used the *Roy Orbison* song of the same name for the soundtrack, along with many other popular songs and a beautifully composed score by *James Newton Howard*. I was invited to the big Hollywood red carpet Premiere for the cast, crew, and critics. The rags-to-riches love story struck a chord in the hearts of audiences around the world, and the film was an instant hit.

Pretty Woman is still the most successful romantic comedy in the history of Hollywood.

Many years later, after Garry passed away, I was the President of *the Burbank International Film Festival*. In his honor, I created *The Garry Marshall Spirit Award* to honor Garry and his life-long career. I was happy to give something back to the Marshall family for everything Garry had done for me.

Chapter 16

Top Secret: Scotland Yard

Not long after my *Pretty Woman* experience my agent called to say that a production company was looking for twins to play the infamous English twin gangsters *Ronnie* and *Reggie Kray* (*The Kray Brothers*). It was for a British docudrama called *Top Secret: Scotland Yard* and our particular episode was titled *The Krays*. Famed director *Alan Parker* had directed a feature-length movie about the infamous brothers called *The Krays* starring the two brothers from *Spandau Ballet*, *Martin* and *Gary Kemp* (although they weren't actual twins). *Alan Parker* also directed music videos for famous recording artists such as *Madonna* and *Pink Floyd*.

The real Kray Brothers   **Jeff & Jerry as the Krays**

Ronald "Ronnie" Kray and *Reginald "Reggie" Kray* were English organized gangsters and identical twin brothers who were prominent from the late 1950s until their arrest in 1968. Their gang, known as *The Firm*, was based in Bethnal Green, where the Kray twins lived. They were involved in murder, armed robbery, arson, protection rackets, gambling, and assaults. At their peak in the 1960s, they gained a certain measure of celebrity status by mixing with prominent members of London society, often being photographed and interviewed on television.

They were born in 1933 in Haggerston, East London. Reggie born was born 10 minutes before Ronnie. Their parents already had a six-year-old son, Charles James, and a sister, Violet, who died in infancy. The Kray household was dominated by their mother, Violet, who remained the brothers' most substantial influence during their childhood. Their father was a rag-and-bone man with a fondness for heavy drinking; his work led him to live a nomadic lifestyle as he traveled all over southern England looking for junk to sell, and even when he was in London, he frequented pubs more often than his home.

Violet was regarded as a minor celebrity in town for giving birth to and raising a healthy pair of twins at a time when the child mortality rate was high among the British working class.

In the interwar period, it was expected that one of the twins born into working-class families would die before adulthood, and it was most unusual that both the Kray twins survived, making their mother the object of much admiration and causing her to have an inflated ego.

There was a feeling among the people in the town that there was an unnatural emotional closeness between the twins and their mother, who shunned the company of others. One of the Krays' cousins who attended school with them, *Billy Wilshire*, recalled: "It's hard to say exactly what it was, but they weren't like other children." The Krays' biographer, *John Pearson*, argued that their mother planted the seeds of the malignant narcissism that the twins would display as adults by encouraging her sons to think of themselves as being extraordinary while fulfilling their every whim.

The influence of their maternal grandfather, *Jimmy "Cannonball" Lee*, caused the brothers to take up amateur boxing, then a popular pastime for working-class boys in the East End.

Sibling rivalry spurred them on, and both achieved some

success. Ronnie was considered to be the more aggressive of the twins, constantly getting into street fights as a teenager. He had a "low IQ," but he was an avid reader who especially liked books about *T. E. Lawrence* and *Al Capone*. *Raban*, a local journalist, attributed much of Ronnie's "savage petulance" as a teenager to his rage over having to hide his bisexual tendencies.

The Kray twins were called to National Service in the British Army in March 1952. Despite a less-than-stellar military career, the Krays adopted an extremely militaristic style. Ronnie called himself *The Colonel* upon release. At the same time, their home at 178 Vallance Road was dubbed *Fort Vallance*. The Krays twins' criminal records and dishonorable discharges ended their boxing careers, and the brothers turned to crime full-time. They bought a run-down snooker club where they started several protection rackets. By the end of the 1950s, the Krays were involved in truck hijacking, armed robbery, and arson, through which they acquired other clubs and properties.

In the 1960s, the Kray twins were widely seen as prosperous and charming celebrity nightclub owners and were part of the Swinging London scene. A large part of their fame was due to their non-criminal activities as famous figures on the celebrity circuit, rubbing elbows with Hollywood celebrities like *Frank Sinatra, Peter Sellers, Joan Collins, Judy Garland, George Raft, Sammy Davis Jr., Shirley Bassey, Liza Minnelli, Dusty Springfield, Jayne Mansfield, Richard Harris*, and others. *The Beatles* and the *Rolling*

Stones were rulers of pop music, Carnaby Street ruled the fashion world, and the *Kray Brother*s ruled London.

In 1960, gambling in clubs was legalized in the United Kingdom, which, for the first time, allowed 'decent' people to gamble openly outside of betting on horse racing. However, the Krays had a "freak show" image that was viewed at the time as perverted sexuality. It was a time when homosexuality was widely considered abnormal, especially in the underworld of the East End — Ronnie made a point of flaunting his relationships with men, which was considered to be quite shocking during this period. Reggie was ostensibly heterosexual, but he had only one known relationship with a woman and was only briefly married; there were also rumors that he had boyfriends as a teenager.

The Krays were not asexual, but the indeterminate nature of their sexuality contributed to their popular image of being, in some vague way, very perverse. The fact that the twins were successful gangsters while not subscribing to the standard heteronormative "hard men" or "lovable rogue" stereotypes associated with their criminal peers, while also rejecting the popular effeminate stereotype of gay men, led to a sense there was something unnatural about them.

By the end of 1967, detectives led by *Leonard "Nipper" Read* had built up enough evidence against the Krays and they were arrested in the hope that other witnesses would come forward once they were in custody. Although Read knew for sure that *Ronnie Kray* had murdered *George Cornell* in the *Blind Beggar* pub, no one had been prepared to testify against the twins out of fear. *'Scotch Jack' Dickson* stepped up and turned in everything he knew about Cornell's murder. The trial lasted for two months and was a media sensation. Such was the

145

demand to attend the trial that seats in the public gallery section of the courthouse were sold on the black market. It was the longest murder trial in the history of British criminal justice. Both were convicted, and Ronnie died in 1995, and Reggie died in 2000.

I played Reggie Kray, and Jerry played Ronnie. It was an exciting experience as both twins had an extremely strong Cockney accent, which Jerry and I pulled off quite well. As an actor, playing a real person as opposed to a fictional one is much more gratifying,

The Rector Brothers as the Kray Brothers interrogate a snitch

but it's also more challenging as I always want to create a character that is as close to the real person as possible. I read two or three books on the Krays and rewatched *Alan Parker's* film to hear how the Kemp brothers did their cockney accents since they are British. My research provided me with this: Ronnie and Reggie were severely psychologically damaged by an unusual mother/son(s) relationship. They also were cold-blooded killers, which is how we played them.

Looking back on that particular acting job and experience I'm extremely proud of how my brother and I portrayed these larger-than-life mobsters, which led to many awards and accolades for the production team. I'm not surprised. It was shot like an actual film and was extremely violent compared to other similar television docudramas. I remember watching it for the first time and thinking the narrator for this project had a very unusual sounding voice, yet it was very interesting and quite captivating. When the show was over, I watched the ending credits to see who the engaging narrator was. I was floored when his name came up on the credits. It was *Johnny Depp*. I heard later that Johnny was a big fan of the *Kray Brothers*, as Johnny is from the UK. He found out about it, called the producers and were ecstatic when he said he wanted to narrate it. It would have been cool to meet *Johnny Depp*, but oh well.

I've played a lot of real-life people in my career, including President *John F. Kennedy (*Bombshell*), William Shatner* (Hustlers, Gamblers & Crooks)*, Donald J. Trump* (Bad President), *Devin Sloane* (Operation Varsity Blues: The College Admission Scandal), *Rear Admiral Spruance* (Sunset Glory: Doolittle's Heroes), *Herbert Marshall* (Feud: Bette & Joan) and a killer on the FOX TV series, *America's Most Wanted* where my performance led to the (real) killers arrest and eventual conviction for murdering two young women.

My next role would take me out of an English Pub on the East End of London and transport me aboard the *Starship Enterprise* to another part of the Galaxy, where a childhood dream would go from science fiction to a dream come true.

Jeff as Reginald "Reggie" Kray

The Kray Brothers make a plan

Chapter 17

Star Trek: The Next Generation

In the early part of my career, I was still doing some extra work here and there to pay the bills between my real acting gigs. One day, *Central Casting* sent me to *Paramount Studios* to be a background performer for a new show on CBS. They couldn't tell me what the show was because it was very hush-hush. I arrived at Paramount and was given directions to one of the sound stages. There was a group of about thirty of us. We were all excited; because of the cloak-and-dagger secrecy, we all knew this would be some major new TV series. I looked around our group, and everyone was about the same age, young, clean-cut, fit, and good-looking. No one was over the age of twenty-five.

We are then asked to stand in a straight line, shoulder to shoulder, as if we were in the military. A guy walked down the line as though he were *General Patton* inspecting the troops. He then started picking people out of the line that would be herded off somewhere (hopefully not to the slaughter). Three or four people had already been selected, and the casting seemed to be very specific. Then the person came up to me. He looked me up and down, and like any good soldier, I kept staring straight ahead. He then says, "Okay, you!" He then said, okay, that's it for now. He picked me and I followed a production assistant to the wardrobe department with the four other actors that had already selected. Woo-hoo, I was in!

We get to the wardrobe department, and one of the assistants took my measurements and asked my shoe size. She said "perfect" and handed me a cool-looking one-piece jumpsuit and a pair of boots. I went into one of the dressing rooms and tried it on. It fit perfectly. I put on the boots and went back to the wardrobe gal. She looked at me, took a couple of pictures, and told me someone from production would take me to hair and makeup and then to the set. "Set for what?" I asked, "Oh, you'll be playing a star fleet cadet on the new TV series, *Star Trek: The Next Generation (Star Trek: TNG)*!" What? Then one of the production assistants came into the wardrobe area and said, "Everyone, follow me!"

He led the five of us into a nearby soundstage and onto the set of the new *Starship Enterprise*. What? It just got better and better! We are then led down one of the ship's corridors. Remember, this was a brand new show, so this was the first time anyone had ever seen these fantastic, futuristic sets. I'm beyond excited. We're finally led into another room off the hallway, which looked very familiar. Then it hit me! It's the ship's transporter room!

The director was already there (the guy who had selected us for the role). The camera crew and lights were all set up and ready to start shooting. The director then tells us that we are going to be "beamed off" the Enterprise. On action, he wanted the five of us to step onto the transporter platform and stand still until he yelled cut! So on action, we do as we're directed, we step onto the platform and stand still. He yelled, "Cut!" and said, "That was great! Do it again." So we do a second take. "Cut! Perfect! Great job! Thank you all very much." They then sent us back to wardrobe, and we changed out of our Star Fleet Cadet uniforms and back into our street clothes. The production assistant came in, gave us our pay vouchers, and said, "Thanks, that's it, you're wrapped!" We worked two hours, in and out, and we still got a full day's pay!

I found out later that Paramount used a photo of us standing on the transporter platform in a marketing gimmick to promote the show. It was part of a *Viewmaster* slide show, which included thirteen other 3-D images from the episode. If you're too young to remember a Viewmaster, never mind. But at the time, that was pretty cool!

Jeff as a Starfleet Cadet beaming off the Enterpise (far left)

I often wonder what happened to the other twenty-five people they called that morning who didn't get cast. Maybe they worked, maybe they didn't. All I know is that I would be seen in the new *Star Trek* TV series onboard the Starship Enterprise. Through some cool visual effects, me and the four other Star Fleet Cadets would be beamed off the ship. Where we wound up, we'll never know, but what I do know is that I love this business! I couldn't wait to brag to all my friends and that ws just the beginning.

The following year, for season two of *Star Trek: TNG*, Jerry and I were cast in the episode, *Up The Long Ladder.* The crew of the Enterprise receives an antiquated distress call from a human colony on *Bringloid V,* which is in danger from solar flares. The colony turned out to have been founded by the crew of the SS *Mariposa,* a freighter launched from Earth several hundred years earlier. There was also a second colony on the planet, made up of clones and in danger of extinction. Two lost 22nd-century Earth colonies, each facing doom in different ways, one by fire, the other by prolonged cloning. To create the cloning colony, CBS cast three sets of twins and two sets of triplets to give the illusion that we were all clones. Visually, it worked great! Although we had no dialogue, we were featured heavily in the episode. This marked my second time working on the show.

For the third season of *Star Trek the Next Generation*, Jerry and I were called back to CBS by famous casting director *Junie Lowry-Johnson* for a guest-starring role in an episode called *Allegiance (Stardate: 43714.1)*. Years later, Junie would cast us both again for an Emmy award-winning episode of the hit police show *NYPD Blue*.

In the episode, we played identical aliens that kidnap *Captain Picard (Patrick Stewart)* and make a duplicate of him. The duplicate commanded the Enterprise while the real Picard was being held captive on the planet surface with three other alien prisoners so the aliens could study their individual intelligence and leadership skills.

Our alien characters, however, are never given a name or a planet; we were just listed in the script as Alien #1 and Alien #2.

When our scripts were delivered from production, we thought it was temporary until they could come up with the name of our race or the name of the planet we came from. Nope. If you look us up on IMDB (Internet Movie Data Base) or the official *Star Trek Compendium*, Jerry is listed as Alien #1, and I'm listed as Alien #2. It's bad enough that I didn't have a character name, but I was Alien #2. And as we all know that #2 is shit.

We were super excited; we finally had a major speaking role on Star Trek! We were then called into makeup to get a complete mold of our heads, which they used to create the alien prosthetics that are custom-made for our particular faces. The head-mold process takes about four hours, and believe me, it's not for the faint of heart. Your entire head is encased in plaster. The makeup guys shove two straws up your nose so you can breathe, as your mouth, eyes, ears, and everything else is covered in plaster. Then, you have to wait an hour for the plaster to dry before they can take it off. You must be cool, calm, and collected to endure this incredibly arduous and uncomfortable process. If you're at all claustrophobic, this isn't for you. I was told many stories how certain actors panicked or freaked out and couldn't finish the process and were summarily let go, and their parts had to be re-cast. No face-cast. No alien. No part. It was not easy, but we got through it.

Eight-time Emmy Award-winning makeup designer *Michael Westmore* created our original alien makeup. Michael was the head of the makeup department, creating over a hundred different aliens through the course of the Star Trek series, and even won an Oscar for the *Jim Carrey* film *The Mask*. Following Star Trek, Michael became one of the industry advisors on the hit

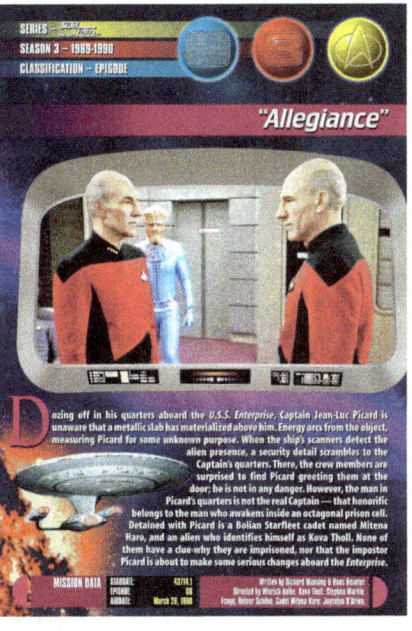

SYFY makeup challenge series, *Face-Off* hosted by his beautiful and talented daughter, *McKenzie Westmore*. The entire Westmore family was legendary in the field of makeup, dating back to 1917

when his grandfather, *George Henry Westmore*, created the very first studio makeup department.

It took two and a half hours every day in the makeup chair to apply my alien prosthetics and just 20 minutes to rip it off at the end of the day. Although Michael designed our alien look makeup artist *Douglas Drexler* applied the makeup for our five days working on the show. Doug had a great sense of humor, and we laughed every minute we worked together, After all, we were stuck in the makeup chair for two and a half hours every day to become the next aliens introduced to the world of Star Trek. "Fishman, he works for scale!" was a running gag. We had a blast. I still run into Doug occasionally at sci-fi conventions and parties.

I remember the first day in the makeup chair because our call time was 4:30 am, so we would be ready for a 7:00 am crew call. FYI, The actor never gets to see what the alien makeup will look like once it's applied that first day. I fell asleep in the makeup chair. Two and a half hours later, they woke me up, saying "you're done!" They held up a mirror before my face. Aaaarrgghhh! I screamed. There was this scary alien staring back at me. The makeup guys loved doing this to see the instant reaction from the actors. Well, they got me all right.

Next was wardrobe. Every alien creature *Michael Westmore* created had to have an outfit or costume. You would think that the makeup and costume departments would work in tandem to make each character. Nope. They were both too busy creating what they needed for up to five or six characters per episode that there was no time to coordinate each look. While the makeup people created the makeup, the wardrobe people created the costumes. Somehow, when they were both eventually put together, they work. It was a miracle, really.

The wardrobe department took our measurements and we were fitted. It turned out that these particular alien costumes were made of rubber. There was a top, a bottom, a belt and two shoes all made of the same material. Underneath the rubber suit, they had us wear a purple one-piece unitard. The costume did not breathe... at all. It was like wearing a wet suit for 12-14 hours daily. It was hot and uncomfortable. The worst part was, if we needed to go to the bathroom, even to urinate, we had to take off the entire costume and put it back on all over again. There was no pee hole—half an hour to take it off, half an hour to put it back on again. And then, you're standing under the hot lights on set for hours at a time.

The rewarding part of the job, despite the uncomfortable make-up and costume, was all of our scenes were with Patrick Stewart. During the different set-ups, I listened to Patrick wax eloquent about his time doing Shakespeare at the *Old Globe Theater* or a million other war stories. I was in Heaven. I also talked quite a bit with *Jonathan Frakes* (*Commander William Riker*), *Michael Dorn* (*Lieutenant Worf*), and *Marina Sirtis* (*Counselor Deanna Troi*). They were all wonderful to work with. While it took us two and a half hours every day for us to get into makeup for five days of work; can you imagine it taking three and a half hours a day to get Michael Dorn into his Klingon makeup every day for eight years? God bless him.

Okay, so we're in costume and makeup and standing on the bridge of the Starship Enterprise next to Patrick Stewart. Pinch me. Am I dreaming? We do our first scene, and it goes great. In another scene, Captain Picard traps us in a force field and says, "Now, how do you like being held in captivity?" Good question, Jean-Luc. What was interesting about our characters (even though we don't have a name) was that our race communicated through mental telepathy. So there was a line in the script where Picard said, "With one look, I was able to communicate with my crew to trap you in this forcefield."

We were ready to shoot the scene, when Patrick turned to the director *Rick Kolbe* (who would eventually direct eighteen episodes of *Star Trek: Voyage*r and eventually falls in love with the shows *Captain Janeway - Kate Mulgrew*). Patrick asked the director, "So Rick, exactly what silent look am I supposed to give the crew to tell them to trap the aliens in a forcefield?" Everyone on the set cracks up. Patrick was only half-kidding. Rick turned to him and said, "You'll figure it out"—more laughter.

When you see the episode, Picard looks at Riker, Riker nods and looks at Worf, nods, and presses some buttons on his console. Voila, we're suddenly trapped in a forcefield (we had to pretend to react to it, even though the CGI (computer-generated image) visual effect would be added much later in post-production.

At the end of the scene, Patrick Stewart said, "Now, how do you like being held in Captivity?" At which point we both look at each other terrified and humiliated and Picard signaled (with a another look), to release us from the forcefield. He then said, "Now, get off my ship!" and we both disappear in a cool (CGI) visual effect.

Where we went, we still don't know. That was the second time I was beamed off the Enterprise to some unknown planet or location never to be seen or heard from again.

Following that scene on the Enterprise bridge, we still had one more scene to shoot on the planet's surface in the holding cell. The TNG crew then broke for lunch. Jerry and I went to the studio commissary to get some food. You should have seen the look on everyone's faces when we walked in as Alien #1 and Alien #2. We turned a few heads. When I passed one table, I could overhear one employee saying to the other, "They must be working on Star Trek." We weren't the only ones. There were a lot of other actors in various costumes and assorted wardrobe from different shows and movies eating lunch. It was a pretty weird scene. Imagine walking into the commissary in the '60s and seeing *William Shatner* (*Captain Kirk*),

Leonard Nimoy (*Mr. Spock*), and *DeForrest Kelly* (*Bones*) sitting there eating a tuna fish sandwich.

To this day, when I'm a celebrity guest at a Star Trek convention, the fans see my pictures with me in my rubber suit and alien makeup, and they all remember the episode and my character. "Hey, you're alien #2!" To this day, I believe that I'm the only principal actor in the history of *Star Trek* to play three different characters in the same Star Trek TV series. I should reach out to the *Guinness Book of World Records*.

To Boldly Go Where No Man Has Gone Before

William Shatner was one of the most iconic and best-known actors in the world of Science Fiction, Fantasy, and Horror. He played *Captain James Tiberius Kirk* in the most popular, longest-running franchise in the history of film and television, the classic sci-fi series *Star Trek*. Unless you've been living under a rock or lived your whole life in Siberia, you know Star Trek and the legendary adventures of Captain Kirk and his crew onboard the *Starship Enterprise NCC-1701*.

For those who don't, here's a brief history. *Captain Kirk* was a strong, handsome, charismatic, intelligent, and fearless captain of an interplanetary starship whose five-year mission was to explore space, seek out new life and new civilizations, to boldly go where no man has gone before. Each episode, Captain Kirk would discover new worlds, battle new aliens and have sex with a different alien species or one of the female crew members. He indeed was a new breed of hero that millions of fans around the world adored and for good reason. Captain Kirk stood for what was right in the Universe and kicked the ass of anyone (human or alien) who posed a threat to the Federation of Planets' code of ethics, honor, and justice. William Shatner was that man, and he brought confidence, sex appeal, and a swagger that audiences had never seen before, especially on television in the 1960s.

Here's a bit of trivia you may not know. William Shatner was not the first choice to captain the Enterprise. The great actor and film star *Jeffrey Hunter* was cast in the original pilot episode for

Star Trek, called *The Cage*. When the series got picked up by CBS, they called Jeffrey Hunter to offer him the lead role of *Captain Pike*. Rumor has it that Hunter's wife at the time, *Joan Bartlett*, said, "Oh no, Jeffrey's a movie star; he's going to need more money to do a TV show." After several strained negotiations, the producers decided to recast the role, and CBS then cast William Shatner. Also,

Jeffrey Hunter **as** *Captain Pike* **with** *Susan Oliver* **&** *Majel Barrett*

almost the entire crew from the Pilot was recast except for *Leonard Nimoy*, who played the science officer, *Mr. Spock*. And the rest is history.

Tragically, after turning down Star Trek, Jeffrey Hunter's career took a downward turn, and on a flight back to Los Angeles, he suffered a stroke and was rushed to the hospital. He recovered several weeks later, but one night, alone at his home, he had another stroke, slipped, fell and hit his head. He was finally discovered, and rushed to the hospital but never regained consciousness and died shortly after. Ironically, if Jeffrey Hunter had not turned down the series, he might very well still be alive today, and the whole history of Star Trek would have been dramatically changed. There probably never would have been a Captain Kirk.

Another bit of trivia you probably didn't know. Guess who owned the Production Company that originally green-lit Star Trek when everyone else in Hollywood turned it down because they didn't get it or understand the potential for the show. The production company was *Desilu,* owned by *Lucille Ball* and her then-husband

Desi Arnaz of *I Love Lucy* fame. Desilu, made up of the combined names Desi and Lucy, produced various other hit shows, including *Mission Impossible*, the classic crime drama *The Untouchables*, *Gomer Pyle*, *The Andy Griffith Show*, *Lassie*, and, of course, *I Love Lucy* to name just a few. So, if it wasn't for *Lucille Ball*, there never would have been a Star Trek universe with all its spin-offs, television series, and motion pictures. Thank you, Lucy!

Star Trek was created in 1965 by *Eugene (Gene) Roddenberry*, known as *The Great Bird of the Galaxy*. He created an amazing world that not only proposed a bright and promising future but also a world where everyone and everything had the right to life, personal beliefs, and, above all, equality. This was an incredible and unprecedented philosophy for a TV show at the time and sharply contrasted the current mood of the world, where racism, exploitation, and human rights are being trampled on as a common way of life.

Gene Roddenberry continued to push these boundaries with bold and inventive scripts and storylines that questioned every ideal in America and the world. When the treatment of African Americans as slaves was still prevalent in the South and segregation between whites and blacks was at its height, he wrote a script that addressed these issues. In the Star Trek episode *Let That Be Your Last Battlefield*, two races of aliens

Gene Roddenberry **Star Trek creator**

with extraordinary powers had been at war for over 50,000 years because they were physically different.

One alien race was entirely black on the left half of their body and white on the right half. The other alien race was the opposite; they were white on the left half and black on the right half. Because of their differences (white and black), this was Gene's way of addressing sensitive racial issues at the time, disguised as science fiction. It was also a way of sneaking these issues into his storylines and making a political or human statement that, typically, the network and studio executives would never have approved due to the explosive content.

Frank Gorshin guest starred in the episode as one of the warring aliens. He would go on to play the very first *Riddler* in the popular TV series *Batman* starring *Adam West*. Years later, Adam and I would co-host

Frank Gorshin and **Lou Antonio Lokai**

the last *Famous Monsters of Filmland Convention* at the *Sheraton Universal Hotel* in *Universal City*. Years later, I would also have the pleasure of meeting *Frank Gorshin* at a *Star Trek* convention in Chicago, where we were both guests. We had some drinks, hung out, and shared a lot of laughs. Frank was also a top comedian and impressionist at the time and had a wicked sense of humor. I also met and became friends with adult actress turned television and film star *Traci Lords* at the same Convention when we all went into the city one night together. *Adam West (Batman)* was also a Convention guest, and we became friends until his untimely death. Other crazy things happened that weekend that I won't go into detail about, but that was definitely a trip to remember.

Rod Serling did the same thing with his groundbreaking television series, *The Twilight Zone*. Like Gene, Rod was an incredibly talented and brilliant award-winning writer who was upset by the racism and injustice that was prevalent at the time. He, too, would write incredible science fiction and fantasy storylines that masked the fact that he was making a political or personal statement about the state of the world and the treatment of human rights. Rod, like Gene, was very vocal in his opinions and fought constantly with the network executives who, many times, were afraid to produce some of their scripts because they felt they were too edgy. Rod was very short in stature at 5' 5" tall and was nicknamed by the studio executives as *The Angry Little Man*.

Rod Serling was born in Syracuse, New York, and his religious upbringing was Jewish. There are many episodes with either holocaust-type storylines or communities run by fascist rulers,

similar to the Nazi regime. Gene also wrote an episode of *Star Trek, Patterns of Force*, where Kirk and Spock beam down to a planet run by alien race similar in dress to the Nazis.

The trademark for *The Twilight Zone* television series was that there was always some incredible twist at the end of every episode that you never saw coming. *The Twilight Zone* also was something that few other shows where at the time: it was an anthology series. That meant every episode had a beginning, middle, and end, making it self-contained. That also meant that each week was a different story and cast. *The Twilight Zone* also introduced and helped launch the careers of many up and coming actors like *Robert Duvall, Charles Bronson, Elizabeth Montgomery, Cliff Robertson, Anne Francis, Montgomery Clift,* and a child actor named *Billy Mumy* who would go on to star in the hit *Irwin Allen* sci-fi series *Lost in Space* and years later on *Babylon 5*.

Another up-and-coming actor at the time was cast by the

name of *William Shatner*, who was one of the few actors to play two different characters in different episodes of *The Twilight Zone*. His most famous episode was *Nightmare at 20,000 Feet*. Shatner played a businessman who had recently recovered from a nervous breakdown. During the flight, the plane encountered a terrible lightning thunderstorm. At one point, Shatner looked out the plane window and saw a mysterious creature on the airplane wing ripping open one of the panels to try and force it to crash. Shatner counldn't believe his eyes, and in a panic, he called for help from the flight crew and uttered the now famous line, "There's something out on the wing!"

But every time the stewardess or ship's captain came and looked out the window, the mysterious creature had vanished, leading everyone to believe that Shatner was imagining things and was having another mental breakdown. The final twist to the episode was that when the plane finally lands at the airport and they take Shatner's character away, the camera slowly zooms in on the wing. We see that one of the wing plates has indeed been ripped open, with the electronic parts exposed just as he claimed.

Like *Star Trek, The Twilight Zone* made an indelible impression on me as a child and further expanded my fascination, obsession and love for the genres of Science Fiction, Fantasy & Horror. As an award-winning writer, director, and producer, Gene Roddenberry and Rod Serling stirred my imagination, introduced me to other worlds, and helped set me on a course through time and space that would change my life forever.

Other genre writers that I grew up reading and inspired me were *Ray Bradbury* (*The Martian Chronicles, The Illustrated Man, Something Wicked This Way Comes*), *Stephen King* (*The Stand, Shawshank Redemption, The Shining*), *Michael Crichton* (*Jurassic Park, Westworld, The Andromeda Strain*), *Dean Koontz* (*Watchers, Phantoms, Odd Thomas*), *Issac Asimov* (*Bicentennial Man, I, Robot, Out of the Unknown*), *Arthur C. Clark* (*2001: A Space Odyssey, Childhoods End, The Twilight Zone*), *Phillip K. Dick* (*Blade Runner, The Minority Report, Total Recall*) and many others. No wonder I'm a sci-fi, horror, and fantasy geek, which eventually led me to become an actor and award-winning filmmaker, making and starring in my own genre films; (*Fatal Kiss*, *Revamped*, and *The End*).

As I mentioned in the previous chapter, I was thrilled to be a guest star on *Star Trek: The Next Generation* (Allegiance) and would forever be part of the the *Star Trek* universe and participate in a variety of *Star Trek* fan conventions worldwide. One of the most popular is held every year in *Las Vegas, Nevada*. Not only do fans get to meet their *Star Trek* idols, but they also get to spend four days in Sin City. It's a bizarre collection of *Star Trek* celebrities, Vulcans, Romulans, Klingons, Andorians, gamblers and strippers. It's a match made in heaven.

I go every year to see *Star Trek* friends, meet the fans, and do some partying. It's like the best High School Reunion ever. Since everyone is so busy working on different TV Shows and movies, it's the one place that everybody congregates to see each other, get bombed and lose a ton of money in the casino. This particular year was the 50th Anniversary of *Star Trek*, a significant milestone in the franchise, and all the top *Star Trek* actors were there, including *Captain Kirk* himself, *William Shatner*.

Some other familiar faces and fan favorites from the original Enterprise crew included *Nichelle Nichols* (*Communications Officer Uhura*) and *Walter Koenig* (*Ensign Pavlov Chekov*). I acted in a sci-fi movie that Walter produced called *Inalienable* which starred the late *Richard Hatch* (*Battlestar Galactica*). We also honored Nichelle at *The Burbank International Film Festival* one year with a lifetime achievement award for acting and the portrayal of a positive role model for African American women. Actress/comedian *Whoopi Goldberg* said that it was *Nichelle Nichols* portrayal of *Uhura* that led to her becoming involved in the entertainment business as a young performer. Unfortunately, original cast members *Nichelle Nichols*, *James Doohan* (*Scotty*), *DeForest Kelly* (*Bones*), and *Leonard Nimoy, (Spock),* have all since passed away.

The Las Vegas 50th anniversary convention also paid tribute to *The Great Bird of the Galaxy, Gene Roddenberry* and the incredible legacy that he had created over forty years ago. Gene's son *Eugene "Rod" Roddenberry* is piloting the ship and carrying on the *Star Trek* tradition his father envisioned over half a century ago. For this anniversary, Rod created a special convention exhibit along with *Creation* (the company that produces these conventions) to honor his father and the series. Rod and I met at a science fiction convention in Hannover, Germany, many years before and became friends. Rod is a really nice and extremely humble guy. Not only is he doing a great job of continuing his late father's legacy, but he is also creating a legacy of his own.

The convention was off the hook! I met *James Doohan's* son, *Christopher,* for the first time who now plays his father's iconic role as *Scotty* on the award-winning web series *Star Trek Continues*, which picks up where the original series leaves off, continuing the five-year mission to go where no man has gone before. Chris even gave me a small sample of some of the actual prop *dilithium crystals* (the energy crystals that power the Enterprise) used on the TV series as a present. They are proudly displayed in my sci-fi memorabilia collection in my office. They are in a small glass vial, so when I show it to people, they think it's crack cocaine at first.

In addition to the rejoicing, reuniting, and revelry, it was a profoundly emotional experience for everyone, including myself. We were all part of the *Star Trek* family, a unique group of actors, writers, directors, producers, special effects people, make-up artists, and production teams that made it the phenomenon it is today. Scientists, astronauts, engineers, astrophysicists, and countless NASA members all share the same story. They grew up watching *Star Trek* and were inspired to become leaders in their fields, whether it's science, astronomy or even space travel.

The Convention started on Thursday and ended Sunday afternoon. Exhausted but exhilerated I'm on *Southwest Airlines* from Las Vegas to Los Angeles on Sunday evening. If you haven't flown them before, Southwest is a cheap, no-frills, no food, get-you-to-where-you're-going airline, which makes trips from LA to Las Vegas almost every hour since it's only a fifty-five-minute flight. The Planes are relatively small, and there are no first-class or business class sections, just coach, and there are no assigned seats; it's first come, first served.

I sit down and relax. Casually I look to my left and there is William Shatner sitting in the window seat, one row up. He's looking at some texts on his phone and facing the window. I figured he didn't want to be recognized as all the passengers were boarding the plane and walking past him. If I were William Shatner, I wouldn't either. On the aisle seat to his right was an attractive Asian woman in her 20s, and the seat between them was empty, but there was a computer case sitting on the seat, probably to discourage anyone from sitting there. I've done that little trick myself to keep someone from sitting there so I have a little elbow room to relax on a flight or in a movie, especially if it has a long running-time or it's a long flight.

Everyone has boarded the plane, and are facing forward. My brain was racing, do I move and try to sit next to him, or do I stay where I am. I've always been a fearless man of action, so I immediately got up, knowing he hadn't seen me sitting in another row. I walked to his row, looked at him with zero recognition on my face of who he was (I'm an excellent actor), and I said nonchalantly (pointing to the empty seat), "Excuse me, is that seat taken?" He looked at me momentarily, graciously said no, and moved his computer case. But I couls tell he probably would rather not have anyone sit there. So I thanked him and sat down without saying another word to him.

We're about ten minutes into the air, and a young female flight attendant asks us if we want something to drink. We all order and the flight attendant asks if I had fun in Las Vegas; I say, "Oh yeah, it was a great trip!" then she says, "What were you doing in Las Vegas?" and I say, "Oh, I'm an actor and I was one of the celebrity guests at the Star Trek Convention." Suddenly, I instantly felt Bill's unease, "Shit, here we go"... Again, I am completely ignoring him and made no mention of who he was to the flight attendant. I figured if she didn't recognize him, I wouldn't bring it to her attention.

She then says, "Oh, which Star Trek series were you on?", I sensed more of Bill's unease. I said, "I was on an episode of "Star Trek: The Next Generation", and she said, "Oh, that one was my favorite!" Whoops, wrong answer. She probably never even saw the original series and was completely oblivious to who was sitting next to me. So we ordered our drinks, and another 20 minutes passed, and I still hadn't said a word to Shatner. I could tell he was thinking that I knew who he was and wondering how long it would be before I start chatting him up. That was my master plan, but I needed a good opening line.

I've already had a few drinks by this time, was feeling pretty cocky and I looked out the window next to Bill and said in a worried tone, "There's something out on the wing!" There was no reaction for a brief moment, then a slight smile, then a chuckle and a laugh. Bill said, "Good one!" I now turned to him and said, "I'm sorry Bill, I couldn't help myself" and he said, "Right." I then held out my hand and said, I'm Jeff Rector, he shook my hand and I continued the conversation as a peer, not a geeky fan.

"We haven't actually met, but we've done a lot of Star Trek conventions together, and I used to ride horses in your *Hollywood Charity Horse* show every year, then he said, "Oh really," and I said, "It's a great charity event, I was proud to participate and show my support, and it's a pleasure to meet you finally," and he said "Likewise." At that point, I could tell that he was finally relaxed, realizing that I wasn't some fanboy who would talk his arm off about Orion Slave Girls, tribbles, or what it was like to work with *Leonard Nimoy.*

We chatted briefly, and not wanting to be too intrusive, I turned back toward the front and didn't say another word to him for the rest of the flight, (which I'm sure he appreciated). We landed in Burbank, and as I got up to leave, he smiled and said, "Nice to meet you, Jeff," and I said, "Nice to meet you too, Bill," and that was it; I got to share a flight and have a laugh with *Captain Kirk.* You're a class act, Bill; God bless you for the countless charity work you do, the people you've inspired (including me), and all the years of entertaining work in film and television.

Years later, I would have the opportunity to play my hero, when I was cast to play William Shatner in a docudrama for *HBO MAX* called *Hustlers, Gamblers and Crooks.* In 2006, William Shatner hosted a popular game show that ran for one season called *Show Me The Money. Hustlers, Gamblers, and Crooks* did a segment that featured game show contestant, *Bob Glouberman* who won $890,000 on the show. So we recreated that episode with me playing Shatner, *David, Moskowitz* played Glouberman and two professional dancers played the shows *Money Girls.* It was a dream come true to play one of my childhood heroes.

What was interesting about the episode was that even though *Bob Glouberman* won the $890,000 prize money, he was never paid by the production company because the episode he won the money on never aired since the show was canceled by the network. Contractually, they didn't have to pay any prize winnings until the episode was officially shown on the air.

Jeff as *William Shatner*

was officially shown on the air. Welcome to Hollywood, Bob! When *Hustlers, Gamblers and Crooks* finally told his true story many years later, Bob finally got his $890,000 from the game show. In the immortal words of Mr. Spock, "Live long and prosper!"

Chapter 19
Live Long and Profit

Star Trek is near and dear to my heart, and I could fill an entire book with all stories and anecdotes from over the years. But there's another topic I'd like to share here. As I mentioned in the last chapter, as a *Star Trek* celebrity, I have been fortunate enough to meet fans, sign autographs, and party with the most incredible group of sci-fi, fantasy, and horror actors, writers, directors, and producers in the known universe.

For over 30 years, I've been a guest at Star Trek Conventions, Comic-Cons, Sci-fi, Fantasy, and Horror conventions, and Memorabilia Collectors Shows all over the world. I've been to London three times, Germany three times, (Bremen, Hannover, and Schweinfert), Chicago, Indianapolis, Detroit, San Jose, Sacramento, Park City, San Diego, Orlando, and many others. One such trip took me to a Star Trek convention in Seattle, Washington.

I'm sitting at my autograph table with about ten different photographs from *Star Trek*, *SLIDERS*, and other sci-fi/horror shows and movies I've worked on. A little kid (about eight years old) comes over to my table. Usually, when a fan comes over, one of two things happens: they hand me a picture of the *Star Trek* or other genre show I've been on, or they choose one of the 8X10 photographs that I'm selling. Photos with a personalized autograph usually sell between $20-$40 depending on the item. When a kid comes to my table, I never charge, I'm just happy to sign a picture for them. I'd never take money from a child (unless they're with their parents who are paying).

I'm there signing pictures when this kid says, "Hey Mista, (that's kid talk for mister), can you please sign this for me? And I say, "Sure kid."

He hands me a *Skybox* trading card with my alien character, which I've never seen before.[4] I had never seen this card before, let alone knew that I was part of this trading card collection.

I was startled at first, but then I got excited; I was now part of this *Star Trek* trading card set. So I said to the kid, "Hey kid, where did you get this?" and he said, "At that table over there," and pointed to a dealer's table selling various *Star Trek* merchandise. The dealer obviously knew I would be a guest at the show, so he was selling my card to convention goers. I said, "Hey, can I keep this? I'll give you a couple of signed photos for it." The kid's eyes lit up, and he said, "Sure!" So I signed a couple of photos for the kid worth $80; he was happy as a clam and went on his way.

After he was gone I walked over to the dealer's table with a brilliant idea. Now, my alien character doesn't look like me because I'm under all the prosthetic make-up, so I said to the dealer, "You don't happen to have any of the trading cards from the *Star Trek: The Next Generation* episode Allegiance, do you? He said, "Oh yeah, I've got a ton of them." So he showed me the cards that were my character and a few other cards that I'm on, and I said, "How much are these?" and he

CONGRATULATIONS

This Limited Edition Card Has Been Personally Signed By

JEFF RECTOR as ALIEN #2 in "Allegiance"

said, $5 each." "How many do you have?" and he said, "About 30", so I asked, "How much for all of them?" His eyes lit up and he said, "I'll sell you all thirty for $4 each." So I paused for a minute

4 Skybox is a trading card company that signed a licensing deal with Paramount Pictures, allowing them to sell their trading cards with all the various Star Trek characters on them along with the title of the show, the episode title, and the particular characters name on it.

and said "I don't know…" "I'll give you $3 each and said okay. So I gave him $90, thanked him, and took the cards to my table.

I signed all the cards and started selling them at my table for $20 each. They sold like hotcakes. Remember, these are collectible trading cards; if you have the actor's signature, they are worth much more money to trade or resell on the Internet. Later, the dealer walked by my table and saw the signed cards for $20. He gave me a look like I just killed his grandmother. I shrugged like, oh well. It wasn't my fault he didn't know who I was. I did feel kind of bad, but what are you going to do? An alien's gotta make a buck.

For my next project I would beam off the Starship Enterprise and work with one of the top action stars in Hollywood, *Jean-Claude Van Damme*.

Chapter 20

Double Impact

It's the early 90's and my agent *Don Gerler* called me to say they were looking for a photo double for *Jean-Claude Van Damme* for his new action film for *Columbia Pictures* called *Double Impact*. In the movie, Jean-Claude played identical twins who were separated at childbirth. Both babies were born in Hong Kong, but one was whisked away to America and raised in Beverly Hills with a silver spoon in his mouth, while the other sibling remained in Hong Kong growing up on the gritty streets and becoming a smuggler and drug dealer. Both twins were raised in martial arts and became excellent fighters.

The casting director was ideally looking for twins to photo-double Jean Claude and to act with him in the scenes involving his twin brother. The camera would be behind and over one of the twins' shoulders, focusing on Jean-Claude and his dialogue. They would shoot the scene one way, then Jean-Claude would switch into the other twin's wardrobe, and reshoot the same scene with Jean-Claude's dialogue as the other twin brother. When both scenes were edited together, it seamlessly looked like Jean-Claude was talking to his identical twin brother. It's an old trick to give the illusion of twins using only one actor playing both roles.

I give Jean-Claude a lot of credit; he not only had to memorize the dialogue for both characters but also be able to switch back and forth between each character to believably portray two distinctively different individuals. That's a tough job for the most seasoned actor, but he pulled it off brilliantly. I still believe that Double Impact is Jean-Claude's best film in his illustrious career as a martial arts action star.

My twin brother Jerry and I were the perfect fit. We were the same height as Jean-Claude, 5'10", and the same general physique, but of course, Jean-Claude was more muscular and built due to his extensive martial arts and daily workout regimen. Even when we were shooting in Hong Kong, he was in the gym every day stretching, training, and working out. Even to this day, I have never had the sort of focus to train that hard and consistently, even though I, too, studied martial arts (Tae Kwon Do). He was at the height of not only his personal fitness but also his popularity as an international action star.

The original casting director was *Miguel Sandoval*, a working actor in his own right. Shortly after I was hired, he left the production to star in another film but they called me in to be interviewed by the director, *Sheldon Lettich*. Sheldon was a great guy, a well-respected director, a member of the Writer's Guild, and a former marine. He had seen some action when he served in the *Vietnam War*. Sheldon was a radioman for the Marines, and one day, he got cut off from his platoon and almost got ambushed by the enemy but was able to narrowly escape with his life. You can read about Sheldon's life in his book, *Sheldon Lettich: From Vietnam to Van Damme*. Sheldon had not only written the script for *Double Impact* but had worked with Jean-Claude on two previous films, *LionHeart* and *Bloodsport,* and would direct three other movies with him, *Hard Core, Legionnaire,* and *The Order.*

Sheldon explained they needed a photo double and that the job would work out of the country in Hong Kong for two to three months. Let me think: am I available to work on a big-budget *Columbia Pictures* feature film in another country with union wages and benefits and doubling for one of the world's top action stars? Hell yeah! I told Sheldon I would be thrilled to do it, and he said great! The next step would be to meet Jean-Claude and get his approval. Miguel was replaced later by casting director *James Tarzia*, who would cast many of Sheldon's films over the years.

The following week, I was called back to the Casting Director's office to meet with Jean-Claude. I have to admit, I was a little nervous, but the moment of truth arrived, and I met with Jean-Claude. He was really nice. After introductions and some pleasantries, I shut up and let him do most of the talking. Both Sheldon and I just sat there and listened. Jean-Claude told me everything I already knew, so I just sat there patiently and smiled. We talked about the doubling aspect of the job, and Jean-Claude said that he has a very

Jeff as Jean-Claude's photo double

specific kind of walk and could I imitate it. He got up, walked across the room, returned and asked, "Can you do that? He was right; he did have a very distinctive walk where he would move his hips as he walked with a confident, cool, macho swagger, which was another reason that, besides being a great action star, he was also considered a sex symbol.

I'm a very quick study, so I got up, walked across the room, moved my hips like he did, then turned around and returned. He watched me intently every step of the way. When I walked back, I looked at him and said, "How was that?" There was silence. He looked at me, then looked over at Sheldon, who nodded, and then he looked back at me, laughed, and said, "That was pretty good!" That broke the ice. The rest of the interview went great, and we shared a few laughs as we both have a great sense of humor. At the end of the meeting, Sheldon thanked me for my time, said they were meeting with a few other people, and they would be in touch, which was usually the kiss of death.

Surprisingly, my agent called the next week and said they wanted to meet with my twin brother and I, which we did. The interview was short and sweet. Once again, the casting director said the familiar line, "We'll be in touch." I waited in angst for the next week or so before my agent finally called and said that Jean-Claude really liked me, and although he hadn't met my twin brother Jerry (since he was not at the first meeting), we had the gig. Woo-hoo! A three-month SAG (Screen Actor's Guild) contract, which meant first-class airfare, 5-star hotel accommodations, and a daily perdium (money paid daily for food and expenses). The pay was fantastic, and I'd be working for *Columbia Pictures* alongside one of the world's top action stars. It was a dream come true and my first major studio contract!

We weren't due to start shooting the film for another month as they had just begun the casting process for the other leads and supporting characters. I was surprised when my agent once again called and said they requested me to "read" with the auditioning actors, and I would be paid accordingly on a daily rate.[5] I was thrilled; not only did I have a guaranteed acting job for the next three months, but I was also getting paid extra money to be part of the casting process for a major motion picture.

A "reader" can read various parts in the audition process, whether it's a male or female character, young person or old, etc. They are just reading or giving the lines to the other actors to cue their dialogue. I had never done this before, so I was excited but didn't know what to expect. When I arrived at the casting office, I was surprised to see Jean-Claude there; I assumed he'd be reading with the leads, and I'd be reading with the supporting roles but the director wanted me to read with everyone, even the lead roles opposite Jean-Claude. Basically, I played Jean-Claude's part as I read with all the actors, both men and women. I had a ball! Well-known actors and actresses that I had loved watching for years on television and motion pictures came flooding in with the hopes

5 A "reader" reads with the auditioning actors so that the casting director can focus solely on the actor's performance and not be distracted.

of getting cast as this was going to be a major film for *Columbia Pictures*.

One day, I would read opposite beautiful female actresses to play Jean-Claude's love interest; another day, I'd read with actors auditioning to play the bad guys. I remember seeing all these name actors, leading men from television and film, some of my all-time favorites coming in to read, and I thought, how cool to be, getting paid to play Jean-Claude's role and read with all these recognizable stars. They were all excellent actors, but some were more right for the role than others. One day when Jean-Claude wasn't there; it was just me and the director *Sheldon Lettich* in the casting session. I remember one actor in particular, *Robert Foxworth*, who was well-known for movies and TV shows. I read with him, and thought, wow, he was great! He had the right look since the role called for an ex-military badass, the "Chad" (Beverly Hills Van Damme) character's mentor and confidant.

After he was finished reading, Sheldon thanked him for auditioning, and he left. Sheldon turned to me and said, "What do you think?" I said, "I thought he was one of the best so far. Are you going to call him back in?" Without missing a beat, Sheldon said, "No, he's a television actor." Wow, that was an eye-opener; even though he was right for the role and was an excellent actor, he was perceived as a television star, not a movie star. It was a valuable lesson for me. If you do a lot of movies, you're a movie star; if you do a lot of television, you're a TV star; if you're on a Soap Opera, you're a Soap star; and if you do a lot of commercials, you're considered a commercial actor or actress. All very different, with different levels of respect in Hollywood.

It's a funny thing: if you're a movie star, you can pretty much do everything; if you're a TV star, it's more difficult to make the cross-over into movies, and if you're a Soap star or a commercial star, it's going to be even more challenging to get into films. That said, you can make a lot of money doing commercials or acting in a long-running Soap Opera. I don't know why it works that way; it just does. Being a movie star carries a certain gravitas and prestige that TV, Soaps, and commercials don't have.

A friend of mine was a Soap Star in New York on *All My*

Children; he was making six figures a year on that show for many years and became a multi-millionaire, but he wasn't happy because he wanted to do movies. He told the producers he didn't want to renew his contract so he could do feature films. He landed the role in one feature film and did a great job, but the movie was a dud at the box office, and he got blamed for it since he was the star. After six months of being unemployed, he returned to the network and asked if he could come back on the soap, and because he was a nice guy and had an extensive fan base, they said yes. Other actors and actresses without that clout haven't been so lucky. Once they leave a show, they're pretty much persona non grata, or the Hollywood translation; you're done!

Jeffrey Lewis **as** *Frank Avery*

The role of *Frank Avery*, Jean Claude's mentor, went to film star *Jeffrey Lewis*, who worked with *Clint Eastwood* on the *Any Which Way But Loose* series of films and would later work with Sheldon again on *Only The Strong*. Jeffrey is also the father of Academy-Award-nominated actress *Juliette Lewis*. Although Jeffrey had done a lot of television, he was predominantly known as a movie star. Years earlier, when I was a tour guide at *Universal Studios*, I would sneak into the sound stages and onto the sets to watch the filming. One day, I was on set, and they were shooting a TV movie, and there was a hostage situation; the bad guys' leader was none other than Jeffrey Lewis, and I recognized him instantly.

The director yelled action, and Jeffrey holding, a machine gun steps up to the hostages and says, "Okay, nobody moves!" then the director yells cut! and I thought, oh, it must be a rehearsal because

Jeffrey certainly could do it better than that. Then the director yells, "Okay, great job, Jeffrey, it doesn't get any better than that, moving on! That was it; they moved on to the next scene. I thought that's the difference between TV movies and theatrical movies; TV movies aren't as good, and the acting doesn't have to be as strong. Jeffrey was a real hoot to work with, and since Jean-Claude and Jeffrey had so many scenes together we had a lot of laughs.

We were in Hong Kong from October 1990 through December. What a great time! It was amazing! At the time, I was

View of downtown Hong Kong from my hotel room

single, but Jerry had a girlfriend. Hong Kong was a melting pot of the most beautiful women in the world. I dated two women from Hong Kong, one from Australia and one from England (the UK).

During production, when we weren't filming in Hong Kong (Kowloon Harbor), we were shooting on an island off the coast where there was a very large abandoned hotel we used for a number of locations. We had to take a boat with the production crew just to get to the island set every day (about an hour and a half ride). Eventually, they let us ride on the private boat commissioned for Jean-Claude and the other stars which was smaller, faster and could make the trip in under an hour. We filmed at that location for about two weeks. Scenes were shot on the beach when the bad guys stormed the hotel in a sneak attack. They landed a helicopter on the beach for the surprise assault; while the action scenes took place in the surrounding dense jungle, and still others were shot in the abandoned hotel, which used to be a high-end vacation resort many years earlier.

My brother and I made so much money on the film that we decided to do something nice for our parents since they had always been supportive of our careers. We decided to surprise them and fly them to Hong Kong for a week's vacation on us. We put them up in our hotel, which was a beautiful five-star OMNI Hotel right on Kowloon Bay. My room was on the 17th floor, so I had an amazing view of the bay and surrounding area. At night, the view was even more spectacular.

When our parents arrived at our hotel, Jerry and I went downstairs to greet them. No sooner had we hugged and welcomed our parents to Hong Kong than a cab pulled up, and Jean-Claude

Joan and Harlan Rector arrive in Hong Kong

got out. The timing was perfect. We introduced our parents to Jean-Claude and we all took pictures together. They were elated.

While they were in town, we decided to take a side trip to Macau, a small island off the coast of Hong Kong. It is primarily known for its world-renowned gambling and casinos. Wanting to really show our parents a good time, we jumped on a boat to Macau.

I have to tell you that I'm not the world's best gambler, but I'm also not the worst. At the time, I enjoyed playing back jack, and the Casino mainly consisted of gambling tables with dealers, not the hundreds of slot machines that you usually find in Las Vegas.

American dealers are generally more friendly than foreign ones. The Russians and Asian dealers both have extremely icy demeanors and most certainly don't want to be your friend. They are there for one reason and one reason only. TO TAKE YOUR MONEY! Their job is to make as much money for the Casino as possible and don't give two shits how much you're losing. Some of them even seem to take pleasure in taking your hard earned money. It's hard to tell if a dealer is Russian or American until you start talking to them or notice that their name tag says, Olga or Gregor.

Asian dealers may be the most wonderful people in the world, but when they are dealing at a card table in a Casino, they are merciless. Why am I telling you all this? When we landed in Macau and walked into the Casino, all the dealers were Asian. After all, we were in Macau, an Asian Province. Needless to say, I lost a lot of money that night. It didn't matter which table I sat at; they kept cleaning me out. But we all had a great time, and my parents loved it, so that was good enough for me. The best rule of thumb when gambling is don't bet more than you can afford to lose!

Production on Double Impact went great; everybody on the shoot did a great job, and we all became one big happy family. This was not always the case, however. Many productions have ended in disasters or horrible experiences. You can't wait for some shoots to end so you can get out of there. "Who do I have to fuck to get off this picture?" Not this one. We were having the time of our lives!

Since we were his photo and acting doubles, we worked closely with Jean-Claude's stunt and fighting doubles. Jerry and I would double Jean-Claude for the acting portions, a French martial artist named *George Bejue* doubled Jean-Claude for the fighting sequences (when Jean-Claude was fighting his twin brother), and *Mark Stefanich* doubled Jean-Claude for any of the dangerous stunts. Jean-Claude did many of his own stunts and preferred to do them, but the production insurance company wouldn't allow him to do certain things. If, for some reason, he got hurt (as many actors do sometimes), it would completely shut down production, costing hundreds of thousands (to millions of dollars) in delays. They couldn't afford that, so a stunt double had to be used to protect the

Jeff hanging out with some of the martial artists and stunt doubles

studio's investment in the production.

George Bejue was a great guy. He worked with Jeanne-Claude on many of his films, including *Universal Soldier* and *Lionheart*. George was skilled in a variety of martial arts, including *Jeet Kun Do*, *Karate*, *Kung Fu*, and kickboxing. George was also trained in a variety of hand weapons and weight-lifting and was the catering chef on *National Treasure* with *Nicolas Cage*. I just found out recently that George passed away in an untimely death in 2022. We miss you, George; I'm sure you're up in Heaven right now, sparring with *Bruce Lee* (Enter The Dragon), *Pat Morita* (The Karate Kid), and *David Carradine* (Kung Fu). A bit of Trivia: I co-starred with *David Carradine* in his last film before he died on

Jeff, Jean-Claude and George

location in Thailand.

As Jean-Claude's photo double, I was also friendly with the martial arts fighters and the other stunt people on the film who would double the other actors, since this was a major action film. Stunt people tend to be a little crazy to do what they do without worrying about getting seriously injured or even killed on a daily basis if something goes wrong. But they also get paid a shit-load of money! I have a lot of respect for what they do and how they have to stay in top physical shape to pull it all off. There was also a lot of drinking. Almost every night, we'd go out partying with the stunt guys, especially when we had a day or two off. It got pretty crazy. But everyone was professional and was ready the next day to go to work.

One stunt was a high fall from the top of a freight loading crane 150 feet above the ground onto an airbag. It's the biggest stunt in the movie. At the end of the film, Jean-Claude kicks the bad guy off the top of the crane. *Dicky Beer* was the stunt man, and if he missed the airbag or didn't control his fall, he could easily break

A few of the Hong Kong stunt team

his back or even die. Everyone was on set that night, whether they were working or not to watch. It was spectacular! One take, and it was perfect! You don't want to have to do that one twice. That night we all went out for drinks and I asked him, "What was it like!" he smiled, took a shot of tequila, and said, "Just another day at the office!" we both laughed.

One of the other stunt guys was named *Jordi Casares*; he was pretty well-known in the stunt world. He doubled *Harrison Ford* as *Indiana Jones* and *Pierce Brosnan* as *James Bond* and has now become a top-notch, much-sought-after Stunt coordinator. That night, everybody went to Casa Mexicana for cervezas and tequila shots. Man, did we get lit up!

The other cast members were great, too. *Cory Everson*, a world-renowned bodybuilder and trainer, was cast as Kara, the lead female villain in the movie. Her legs were almost as big as Jean-Claude's. There was a famous scene in the film where she gets him in a scissor lock with her legs, trying to choke him out. She was sexy, beautiful, and one of the sweetest people I've ever met. We became great friends on the shoot.

Jeff gets cozy with *Cory Everson*

Jean-Claude was great too, but he was so busy playing both parts and choreographing a lot of the fight scenes that there wasn't much time to hang out and shoot the shit. One day, we were at lunch during production, and I saw Jean-Claude, so I took my lunch over and sat down across from him. Once I sat down, I realized that the famous pop star *Janet Jackson* was sitting right next to him. She reached out and introduced herself. I shook her hand and said hello. Janet was in Hong Kong for her World Tour. Sitting next to her was her choreographer, whom she would later marry. Jean-Claude was interested in Janet and invited her to the set for lunch. I sat quietly while he and Janet talked. After a while, Jean-Claude excused himself to get back on set, so I was left sitting across the table from Janet. She asked what I did on the production, and I told her that I doubled Jean-Claude for the acting portion of the film.

She thought that was fascinating. She then asked me if I

wanted to come see her perform that night at her concert. Would I? Hell Yeah! I told her I'd be thrilled, and true to her word, I had a VIP ticket waiting in my name at the venue. She was amazing! It was a huge concert venue in downtown Hong Kong with thousands of adoring fans. Seeing that kind of adoration from fans halfway around the world was surreal. As I said, this particular job was one of the most amazing experiences of my life.

As the production lasted for over three months, we celebrated three holidays in Hong Kong: Thanksgiving, Halloween, and Christmas. We would have spent New Year's Eve there, too, except that the producers wanted to get everyone home for the New Year for many reasons, including production costs, which were already way over budget. Interestingly, there is a small part of town in Hong Kong that is very Americanized; they even had a restaurant called *California*. So, if we ever got tired of Asian food, we could go to *California* and get a cheeseburger and fries, spaghetti, Caesar salad, or a chocolate shake. There was also a huge floating restaurant in

Jeff with Cory and *Janet Jackson*

A vampire and his mummies on Halloween

the middle of Kowloon Bay called, wait for it, *The Jumbo Floating Restaurant*. We had many delicious dinners (and drinks) there as well. It was pretty amazing. You'd have to take a boat from the shore

The Jumbo floating restaurant in Kowloon Bay

to get there and back.

Halfway through production, we were told that the production was over budget and that some of the movie would be filmed back in Los Angeles on a sound stage. That was fine with me; after three months abroad, I was ready to get back home. All through production, Sheldon kept saying he was going to give me a speaking role in the film for all the hard work that I had done from casting through production. He said there would be a short scene in a karate dojo with a karate student smart-mouthing Jean-Claude as the karate instructor and that he wanted me to play the role. I told him that would be amazing and that I would really appreciate it. When we finally got to LA, Sheldon informed me that Jean-Claude had promised that role to his agent (*Jack Gilardi*) for his son to play and that was that. Oh well. Welcome to Hollywood, Jeff!

I still think that Double Impact was, and still is, one of Jean-Claude's best films of his career. Spending three months in a foreign country with so much to see and experience was a once-in-a-lifetime opportunity. The delightful interaction with people from all over the world was both exhilarating and educational. Meeting and hanging out with musical icon Janet Jackson, doubling for Jean-Claude Van Damme, one of the world's top martial artists, and working with a seasoned and compassionate actor like Jeffrey Lewis was a true joy. May every actor be able to have an experience like that at least once in their career. In the meantime, I keep my faith and remain excited about my next project (whatever that might be) as I continue my journey through life.

On May 28th, 2019, a special Collector's Edition of Double Impact was remastered and released on Blu-ray. I was interviewed and appeared in the Bonus Material section of the DVD, along with commentary from the director, Sheldon Lettich, the stunt coordinators, production people, and other stars from the film. It looks great, and I am so proud and honored to have been a part of it. To this date, it is the most fun, memorable, and lucrative acting experience in the 45+ years of my career. Thank you, Sheldon and Jean-Claude, and a very special thanks to Columbia Pictures and all the fantastic cast and crew that made this film and this experience so incredible.

Cory, Jeff and *Elana Shaw*

Jeff in the jungle ready for action

Jean-Claude with the director

Jeffrey Lewis, Bolo Yeung, Alana Shaw and Hong Kong stunt team

Jeff with *Kamel Krifa*

Jeff with Director *Sheldon Lettich*

Jeff parties with *Peter Malota, Jordi Casares* and friend

Chapter 21

Father Dowling Mysteries

My twin bother Jerry and I were on a roll booking a lot of twin jobs together. Our next gig was a guest-starring role on the hit TV series *Father Dowling Mysteries*. Father Dowling was a top-rated murder/mystery TV series in the style of *Murder She Wrote* and *Diagnosis Murder* and ran on ABC from 1989-1991. The show starred *Tom Bosley* (Mr. Cunningham on *Happy Days*) and *Tracy Nelson*, the daughter of the famous singer/songwriter and actor *Rick Nelson* (Ozzie and Harriet). The show's premise follows an amiable, inquisitive Chicago Catholic Priest (Bosley) who moonlights as a detective, solving murders, abductions, and other mysteries, assisted by a street-wise, lock-picking nun named Sister Stephanie (Nelson).

Tom Bosley and *Tracy Nelson*

The episode was called *The Devil in the Deep Blue Sea* and starred a trendy actor named *Michael Champion*, who played the devil. He was amazing. Not only was he a great actor, but he also sang and played the piano, which was written into the script since the devil owned a nightclub called *Club 666*. Get it? So we were his bad guy, twin hitmen. He sends us on a mission to kill Sister Stephanie's brother, who owes him money and has reneged on his bet with the devil. It was a really cool episode and was directed by *John Kretchmer*, who would cast me many years later in an episode of *SLIDERS* with *Jerry O'Connell* and *John Rhys Davie*s and as the *Mayor* of Neptune in an episode of *Veronica Mars* with *Kristen Bell* and *Enrico Colantoni*.

Jeff and Jerry as the Devil's Hitmen

Ever since I was a tour guide at *Universal Studios*, I've always felt that Universal was my home studio and will always have a special place in my heart. One day as a tour guide, I was driving around on the back lot giving my tour, and I said to myself, one day I'm going to be on this back lot as a principal actor, not as an extra or a tour guide. Well, here I was, on the backlot in Stage #5, starring in an episode of *Father Dowling* Mysteries. The great *Walt Disney* once said, "Dreams can come true if you have the courage to pursue them!" He's right, Dreams can come true if you believe in yourself, follow your dreams, and be persistent.

My next job would take me from a serious drama to a sitcom (situation comedy) on a show called *Normal Life*. There I'd meet the original Valley Girl, *Moon Zappa*.

Chapter 22

Normal Life

After guest-starring on Father Dowling Mysteries, my twin brother Jerry and I were cast on a new sitcom called *Normal Life*. The Show starred *Moon Unit (Moon) Zappa*, and her real-life brother, *Dweezil Zappa*, whose father was the legendary and controversial singer, songwriter, and musician *Frank Zappa*. In the show Moon and Dweezil play brother and sister (big stretch), with comedic actress *Cindy Williams* (*Happy Days*, *Laverne & Shirley*) playing their TV mom and actor *Max Gail* (*Barney Miller*) playing their father.

It was a coming-of-age comedy about Moon and Dweezil growing up. In Episode #3, titled *Two Timin'*, I randomly meet Moon in public, and we start dating. Moon tells her best friend, Prima (*Bess Meyers / Friends*), that she's met this incredible new guy and thinks, "He's the One!" In the meantime, Prima meets my real-life twin brother Jerry, and they start dating. *Cindy Williams* randomly sees Jerry and Prima together on a date and thinks it's me and that I'm cheating on Moon. Hence the title *Two Timin'*.

When Cindy tells Moon that her best friend Prima is seeing her boyfriend, Moon lets Prima have it, only to realize that Prima didn't know her new boyfriend was also Moon's new boyfriend. So Moon and Jess concoct a plot to get even with my character (Jim) and plan a horrible and embarrassing date, not knowing that my twin brother is involved and that I'm completely innocent. At one point, during the date from Hell, Moon pours a whole glass of ice-cold water on my crotch and says, defiantly, "Ha!" To which I reply, "Are you nuts?" Suddenly, my twin brother shows up because I wanted to introduce him to my new girlfriend.

Moon and Jess see us together, realize what happened, and are completely embarrassed. They both apologize profusely, but it's too late; neither one of us wants to have anything to do with two scheming women who assumed I was a cheater without first talking it out. The episode was hilarious and directed by comedy genius *Greg Antonacci*, an actor, writer, and producer known for such shows as *Boardwalk Empire*, *The Sopranos,* and *Laverne & Shirley*.

Moon Unit Zappa

I have to admit; when I found out that I was going to be playing the boyfriend of the original Valley Girl *Moon Unit Zappa,* and I would be working with her and her brother *Dweezil*. I didn't know what to expect. This was based upon what I knew about their unconventional father Frank and from what I saw and read in the news and what I heard from his music. But once I was on set and talked with them, I have to say, they were the coolest, most down-to-earth, humble, and nicest people I've had the privilege of working with. We laughed a lot and had a great time, and Normal Life is still one of the best experiences I've ever had working on a sitcom.

A little back-story about the Zappa family: as I mentioned,

Frank Zappa

their father was the famous rock star Frank Zappa, who composed rock, pop, jazz, jazz fusion, orchestral and other works; he also produced almost all of the 60-plus albums that he released with his band the *Mothers of Invention* and as a solo artist. His work is characterized by nonconformity, improvisation, sound experimentation, musical virtuosity, and satire of American culture. Zappa also directed feature-length films and music videos and designed album covers. He is considered one of his generation's most innovative and stylistically diverse musicians.

Dweezil Zappa

Dweezil followed in his father's footsteps and became a guitarist, musician, and composer. Exposed to the music industry from an early age, he developed a strong affinity for playing the guitar and producing music. Able to learn directly from guitarists such as *Steve Vai* and *Eddie Van Halen*, Zappa released his first single (produced by Eddie) at the age of 12. In addition to writing and recording his music, *Dweezil* has carried on his father's music legacy by touring with the group *Zappa Plays Zappa*."

Dweezil was a nickname coined by Frank for a funny-looking pinky toe of his wife Gail. At the age of five, Dweezil learned that his legal name was different, and he insisted on having his nickname become his legal name. Gail and Frank hired an attorney, and soon, the name Dweezil became his official name. In the 1980s, Zappa worked as an MTV VJ and was promptly fired after badmouthing MTV on *The Howard Stern Show*.

Moon Zappa was no novice when it came to acting having appeared on the television series *CHiPs, The Facts of Life*, and the films *Nightmares, National Lampoon's European Vacation, Spirit of '76,* and *The Super Mario Bros. Super Show.* As an adult, Moon has worked as a stand-up comic, magazine writer and actress, appearing in an episode of *Curb Your Enthusiasm,* as *Ted Mosby*'s cousin Stacy in an episode of *How I Met Your Mother*, and on an episode of *Roseanne.* In an interview with the *Los Angeles Times*, Zappa said she was working on a book about growing up in her "crazy house". Moon's memoir, *Earth to Moon*, was released in 2024.

Moon first came to public attention in 1982 at 14, when she appeared on her father's hit single *Valley Girl.* The song featured Moon's monologue in "valleyspeak," a slang term popular with teenage girls in the San Fernando Valley, Los Angeles. *Valley Girl* was Frank Zappa's biggest hit in the United States. The song made Moon an instant celebrity. Soon, everyone was using "valleyspeak" and saying famous phrases, such as "Gag me with a spoon," "Grody to the max," or, the most sarcastic and popular of all, "Oh my God!"

According to *Wikipedia*, a valley girl is: "a socioeconomic, linguistic, and youth-subcultural stereotype and stock character originating during the 1980s: any materialistic upper-middle-class young woman associated with unique vocal and California dialect features from the Los Angeles commuter communities of the San Fernando Valley." In subsequent years, the term was broadly applied to any American woman who epitomized frivolity, ditziness, or air-headedness or who prioritized superficial concerns such as personal appearance, physical attractiveness, and excessive materialism over intellectual or personal accomplishment.

Fast Times at Taft High

If Moon Zappa was a "Valley Girl", then I was a "Valley Guy" or "Valley Dude," because I too lived and went to high school in the San Fernando Valley. I went to *William Howard Taft High* in Woodland Hills, next to the city of Tarzana, where we lived, and next to the town of Encino. Tarzana was named after famous author

Edgar Rice Burroughs (ERB), who created the iconic action/adventure character *Tarzan*. ERB owned a 550-acre ranch in the valley (mostly orange orchards and a lot of dirt). ERB would ride his horse from his ranch down to the valley to and from work every day. The town was later named Tarzana in his honor. Flash-forward to 2022. I returned to my roots and became the President and Festival Director for the *Tarzana International Film Festival*. I also created the *Edgar Rice Burroughs Legacy Award*, but that's another story for another time.

Tarzana, Encino, and Woodland Hills were predominantly Jewish communities, so Taft High School had predominantly Jewish students. Growing up in Michigan in a mostly WASP (White, Anglo-Saxon, Protestant) suburb of Bloomfield Hills, I had never met anyone of the Jewish faith, so it was a new experience for me. My best friend was a Jewish kid named *Rick Chudacoff*; he quickly educated me about his religion and their beliefs.

I was a sophomore when we moved to California from Michigan, and most of the kids at school knew each other since elementary school. I was not only an outsider but a Christian who was meeting everyone for the first time. Rick helped acclimate me quickly. A typical running joke and a misnomer at the time was that Jewish women were prudish and weren't very forward sexually. This couldn't be further from the truth.

My first job was at a *Baskin-Robbins* ice cream store in Tarzana. There was an adorable girl named Karen who worked there, and we hit it off right away and started dating. It turned out that she also went to Taft which was a big plus. When things were slow at the store, we'd sneak into the Walk-In (the freezer where they kept all the ice cream) and have sex. The combination of the cold freezer and her warm body was exhilarating. Other nights, I'd come over to her house, and since her bedroom was on the first floor, she'd open her bedroom window, I'd climb in, and we'd "get busy" there. I still find it a miracle that we never got caught since her parents were always home.

Taft was also known for having a lot of celebrities kids attend the school since Tarzana was very affluent and was a popular place for the Hollywood elite to live and raise their families. In my Senior year, I dated *Karen Crane* (a different Karen); she was the daughter of actor *Bob Crane,* who played *Colonel Hogan* on the popular TV series *Hogan's Heroes.* My friend, actor and impressionist *Jim Meskimen*, was the son of actress *Marion Ross* (Mrs. Cunningham on *Happy Days*), and singer/songwriter *Cherie Curry* (The Runaways) was also in my class. NFL football player *Jeff Fisher*, Singer/songwriter Joan Jett, and guitarist *Jane Weidlin* (The Go-Go's) all graduated from Taft just one year before me.

Other Taft celebrity Alumni include *Lisa Kudrow* (Friends), actor/rapper *Ice Cube*, actor *Wilmer Valderamma* (*That 80's Show*), gold medal Olympic diver *Sue Gossick*, saxophonist *Dave Koz*, actor *Justin Bateman*, actress *Maureen McCormick* (The Brady Bunch), NASA astronaut *Kathryn Sullivan*, (the first woman to walk in space), actress *Justine Bateman*, actress *Susan Olson* (The Brady Bunch) and Olympic ice skater *Judi Blumberg* to name a few.

My first two years of High School was in Bloomfield Hills, Michigan, I was in several of the school plays, not because I aspired to be an actor; I just thought it was fun. So, I enrolled in play production at Taft to try more acting as I enjoyed it. I showed up on my first day of class, and the teacher, *Mrs. Cabral*, asked me what I was doing there. I said I signed up for the class, and here I am. She said, "Oh, no, you need to have had a previous drama class as a pre-requisite to be in this class!" I said, "I just moved here from Michigan, so this is my first class." Awkward silence. She said, "Well, you'll have to do an audition to get in here then." Huh? *Mrs. Cabral* then says,

"Okay, who wants to improvise a scene with Jeff?" I'm mortified, and the whole class is staring at me. Without skipping a beat, a cute brunette student named *April Winchell* jumps up. "I will!" April was the daughter of a famous ventriloquist and comedian, *Paul Winchell*. Paul was also an inventor and humanitarian. He named his ventriloquist dummies *Jerry Mahoney* and *Knucklehead Smiff*.

Before I know it, April and I are improvising a comedic scene where I'm a delivery guy bringing her a pizza. Everyone was laughing, and it went great. *Mrs. Cabral* laughs and says, "Okay, you're in!" It all happened so fast that my head was still spinning, but I was in! Woo Hoo! I was in! April literally saved my tuchus (which is Yiddish for butt).

If she hadn't jumped up to help me, or if I choked, or if I wasn't funny, I might not have gotten into the class, and my whole future might be different. I had a secret crush on April after that, but I was shy, and she graduated that year. April has since become one of the top voice actresses in Hollywood doing famous voices for Disney projects like *Duck Tales, Mickey Mouse, Looney Tunes, Toy Story, Who Framed Roger Rabbit*, and countless others. After high school, I think I only ran into April one time. Thank you, April. You changed my life. I will always be indebted to you.

A lot of motion pictures have been shot in the San Fernando Valley, *Planet of the Apes, Boogie Nights, Terminator 2* and the 1982 hit comedy *Fast Times at Ridgemont High*, directed by *Amy Heckerling* (her first feature film). Fast Times was written by *Cameron Crowe* (*Almost Famous* and *Jerry McGuire*) and took place in the San Fernando Valley, but was patterned after Clairmont College in San Diego where Crowe went undercover pretending to be a high school student to write about his experiences.

Fast Times at Ridgemont High became an instant classic, defining every high school comedy before or since. The film also made stars from unknown actors like *Sean Penn, Nicolas Cage, Eric Stoltz, Forest Whitaker, Anthony Edwards, Jennifer Jason Leigh, Phoebe Cates, Judge Reinhold*, and many more. In 2005, the Library of Congress selected the film for preservation in the United States National Film Registry as being "culturally, historically, or aesthetically significant."

The very next year, *Nicolas Cage* would go on to star in another High School comedy called *Valley Girl* (also known as Bad Boyz), directed by *Martha Coolidge* and was loosely based on the tragedy *Romeo and Juliet* by *William Shakespeare*. The film centers on the romance between a valley girl (*Deborah Foreman*) and a city punk (*Nicolas Cage*). It also garnered critical success and was a hit at the box office to help cement Cage as a teen heartthrob.

The Zappa family has made an indelible mark in the music industry, television, and film, especially in decades of pop culture. Sadly, Normal Life only lasted one season and was unceremoniously canceled by CBS.

Normal Life was one of the best and funniest comedies on television at the time. It just goes to show that success isn't always based upon talent, excellent writing, great directing, great producing, great acting, and funny scripts. Oh well. That's Hollywood.

Working on *Normal Life* was great fun with a great cast and lots of laughs, but my next project would be anything but as I was about to embark on my next step up the Hollywood ladder and star in my very first feature film and it wasn't a comedy.

Teen Set
"NORMAL LIFE"

Chapter 23

Street Soldiers

Not long after *Normal Life* was canceled my agent called me to read for an independent martial arts/action film called *Street Soldiers*. I wasn't told much about it except that the basic storyline

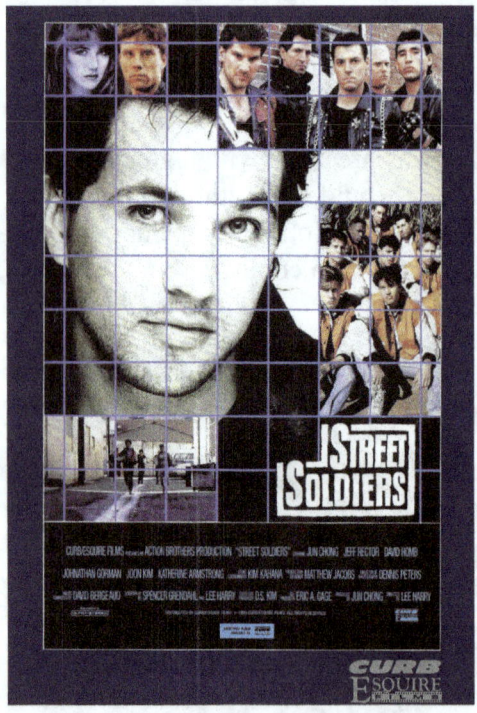

involved two rival street gangs: a gang of high school kids known as the *TIGERS* and a brutal street gang called the *JUDAS PRIESTS* (JP's). I was reading for the lead role: the leader of the JP's whose name was Priest. Get it? So I went in and auditioned. Up until this time, I hadn't played a bad guy before. Since I'm pretty clean-cut, I was always cast as the hero, the cop, the detective, the nice boyfriend, etc.

I didn't know what they wanted, so I wore tight black leather pants, cowboy boots, a black t-shirt, and a black leather jacket to look as tough as possible. Here's a tip for any actors out there: when reading for a movie (not a TV show), wear something as close to the character as possible. If you are reading for a corporate executive, government agent, or lawyer, go in in a nice suit and tie (not blue jeans and a t-shirt, duh); if you're reading for a cowboy, wear blue jeans, cowboy boots, and a cowboy hat if you have one. It's just common sense.

I remember one time I was reading for the boss of a big company; I wore my power suit and tie, and this guy came into the audition wearing swimming trunks and a tank top. I asked him why he hadn't worn a suit. He said he had just returned from the beach surfing and couldn't carry a suit on his motorcycle. I couldn't believe it. I don't care how good an actor he was; he wouldn't be getting that job. Also, it shows a lack of respect for the casting director that you would come in looking like that.

I go into the audition and look as tough as possible and even change my voice to make it sound rougher and scarier. The director was a nice guy named *Lee Harry*. We read through a couple of scenes and he said I did a good job, thanked me for coming in, and I left. The following week, I got a call from my agent, who said that the director wanted to see me again. I went in for a callback.[6] I went back in wearing the same black leather outfit. *Another actor tip. If you get a call back for something, wear the exact same thing that you wore for the original audition. (For ladies), don't change your hair, wear different makeup or a different outfit. They called you back because they liked how you looked and dressed the first time, especially for commercials.

Think about it. The Ad Agency and clients are reviewing your videotaped audition over and over again, along with a ton of other possible actors. They're used to seeing you in the pink dress, the blue suit, khaki pants, whatever. If you go in wearing something different or looking different, they will see you differently. They may not even realize what it was, but something changed, and it could cost you the job. Don't take the chance. ALWAYS wear the same outfit on the callback as you did during the original audition.

This time, he gave me some new scenes to read, and I ended up getting the part. Woo-hoo! The lead in my first film, and as a bad guy, no less. In fact, Lee liked what I wore so much that I wound up wearing my black leather pants, black cowboy boots, and a custom-made black leather vest with studs, chains, and some metal skulls sewn on for good measure. I have to say, I looked pretty badass and

6 A callback is when they call you back in to audition for a second or third time. That means they like you, and you're getting closer to getting the part.

was one of my most enjoyable roles ever.

You can have a lot more fun and make some wild character choices as a bad guy than you can as the hero or good guy and believe me, this guy was an asshole! He had a menacing switchblade that he would whip out in a fight that had brass knuckles on the end, so he'd either cut you with the razor-sharp blade or break your jaw or your nose with the brass knuckles. I did a lot of damage, kicking, punching, and stabbing my adversaries. Like I said, he was a real asshole.

(L to R) *Jude Prest, Joel Weiss*, **and Jeff**

Since it was a martial arts/action film, all the actors went through intensive six-week stunt and martial arts training sessions. The stunt training was done by a Hawaiian stunt coordinator named *Kim Kahana* (who passed away on August 12th, 2024, at the age of 94). Kim was best known for playing *Chongo* on *Danger Island,* which was part of the *Banana Splits* Saturday morning kids show created by *Sid* and *Marty Kroft*. Kim was a real-life badass who served in the Korean War, where he received two bronze stars, a silver star, and two purple hearts for his bravery. Kim was a veteran in the movie business and was *Charles Bronson's* stunt double for many years. He taught us stunt and combat fighting, utilizing not only our bodies but also weapons like guns, knives, and even spears. We even got to do some high falls from about ten feet off the ground. It was pretty cool. Since Kim would be choreographing all the fight scenes, he knew what weapons Lee wanted to have us fight with, and that's what he trained us for. We learned how to do falls, tumbles, and rolls, but most importantly, how to stage a street fight without anyone getting hurt. Or so we thought.

Tae Kwon Do Master *Jun Chong* did the martial arts part of the training. Jun was only about five feet, five inches tall, but you didn't want to mess with him. He would take you out so fast your head would spin. He was also a great guy, and we became good friends long after the movie wrapped. Jun taught us different aspects of self-defense and martial arts and choreographed all the fight scenes, while *Kim Kahana* choreographed all the stunts. The actors that played all the gang members were up to the challenge, and when you see the film, it's all very real looking, not the phony-baloney, chopsocky fighting you see in traditional Japanese martial arts films.

As Priest, I had seven different fight scenes throughout the course of the film. Some fights were with a knife, some with a gun, and some with my fists and feet (punching and kicking). Through Master Chong, I learned the martial art of *Tae Kwon Do*. We did a mixture of martial arts and street fighting to make the fights look more realistic and exciting. Everyone did a great job. One night, when we were shooting, I had a one-on-one fight scene with *Joey Nabor* (one of the Tigers). I'm supposed to back-fist him in the face, but I misjudged our distance, this, after weeks of training and rehearsals and doing the fight scene perfectly time after time. I got too close to him, and I popped him in the nose by accident. He goes, oh my God, my nose! I'm like, oh, I'm sorry, I'm so sorry, Oh my God, it was an accident. I'm sorry!

A violent end for Priest, Jeff's character

After a few minutes, he calmed down, and we reset the fight scene, and we did it again. This time, I have the right distance and do the move perfectly without hitting him, but then it's his turn to punch me in the face. Well, that motherfucker wound up and purposely clocked me right in the mouth with his fist so hard that one of my teeth punched a hole in my lower lip. I'm lucky he didn't break my jaw. So they rush me to the emergency room; I get four stitches in my lower lip and go right back to the set to finish the fight scene. I was pretty pissed off, to say the least. If it was the other way around, I wouldn't have retaliated by punching a fellow actor in the face, especially the star of the movie. It was an accident. But not everybody's the same. He took it personally, and he shouldn't have. But we finished the fight scene and moved on.

I ran into him and his girlfriend many years later, and we laughed. I'm not the kind of person that will carry a grudge for very long. It doesn't serve you to hold onto anger like that; it will eat away at you, and then you're the one who's going to suffer from it the most. Constantly dwelling on how you're going to get back at this person or that person or even just general feelings of animosity and hate will cause more damage to you than the person with whom you want to inflict the pain. When you see our fight scene in the movie, it looks like we were trying to kill each other. Maybe we were.

One of the other JPs was a Brooklyn actor *Joel Weiss*. He was a New Yorker all the way. *Yankees, Mets, Giants*, you name it, he had tickets to all the games. Joel had a very thick Brooklyn accent, which fit well for his particular role. He was cast as "the driver" for the JP's gang ride. The problem was, like most New Yorkers, Joel didn't have a driver's license; in fact, he had never even driven a car before. So he basically lied to the director and told him he could drive, which he couldn't. There is a crucial scene where the JP's car pulls right up to the camera. It's a great shot of the hood of the car with the JP's emblem on it as the car comes into the frame.

Half an hour before the scene, one of the stunt guys says to Joel, okay, time for your driving lesson and takes Joel outside for a crash course (no pun intended) on how to drive a car. He drives the car around the parking lot a few times, and everything seems fine.

They shoot the scene; the camera starts rolling, the director yells action, Joels hits the gas and drives toward the camera, then Joel gets confused. Instead of hitting the brakes, he hits the gas and plows right into the cameraman and his assistant, destroying a $100,000 16mm camera and sending the DP (Director of Photography) and the first AD (Assistant Director) to the hospital. Pretty stupid. This accident should never have happened.

Note to Actors: this is what happens when you lie about having certain skills or abilities when you're auditioning for a role. I saw another instance of this when I was working for *Sandler Tape and Film*. We were casting a commercial for Suzuki Motorcycles. The advertising agency needed eight beautiful blonde models to drive motorcycles across the Bonneville Salt Flats in unison. The first question at the audition was, can you ride a motorcycle? And all the actresses said, oh yes, of course. Sure enough, a lot of them could, and some of them couldn't. They lied about their motorcycle riding experience. One such actress received a callback, so she had her boyfriend show her how to drive a motorcycle. It's not that easy, especially when you are riding on only two wheels; it's not something you can just pick up on a weekend.

We're shooting the women at the callback who had to drive the motorcycle down to a certain mark, turn around, and come back. It was going great until that one actress who lied about her abilities turned around and came back, and she did the same thing as Joel. Instead of slowing down, she accelerated and slammed face-first into a brick wall. Paramedics were called immediately, and she was taken to the hospital. She was lucky she only had a concussion. Thank God she was wearing a helmet, or she would have died instantly. The funny part of the story is she actually got cast to be in the commercial. I think they were afraid of the legal liability, and so they cast her to keep her mouth shut. The shoot was fine because they were just driving straight on the Salt Flats for a quarter of a mile or so. The lesson to be learned here? Don't say you can do something when you can't. Whether it's playing a guitar, swimming in the ocean, scuba diving, or whatever, it may not end well. When you get on the set, and they realize that you can't do what you said you could, it's bad news. They'll probably fire you, and the word will get around to other casting directors that you lied about your abilities. Not good!

(L to R) *Katherine Armstrong*, **Jeff,** and *Joel Weiss*

We finally finished shooting *Street Soldiers*, which was pretty grueling due to a quick shooting schedule with multiple locations, stunts, visual effects, and a lot of fighting. I remember it was the last day of shooting, and we had to pull an all-nighter because we had to shoot out of our locations and couldn't go back and do any pickup shots. *Katherine Armstrong* was the female lead in the movie. She played the girlfriend of *David Holm*, who was the eldest of the Tigers gang. Catherine was very cute and very talented. I was flirting with her during production, but it was obvious she wasn't interested in me, which was fine. But the final night, we were both lying in the back of a van that was used in the movie for a character called *Wheelchair Willie*. It was about six o'clock in the morning, and we were exhausted after filming all night, and we still had one more scene to shoot together. So we're lying there and just talking. I told her what a great job she did, and she complimented me as well. We're looking into each other's eyes, and the next thing I know, she leans over and starts to kiss me. Nothing happened beyond that; we just laid there kissing each other. I guess there was some attraction after all. For whatever reason, she didn't want to pursue anything, but that was a wonderful moment in time. I never saw her ever again.

After we finally wrapped that morning, everyone went their separate ways. I'll always be grateful to Lee for giving me that role

Jeff and his street gang The Judas Priests

and that amazing opportunity. I had finally fulfilled a childhood wish. I was a movie star.

Street Soldiers was the first of many independent films I would star in that were referred to as B-movies at the time. Just ask another B-Movie star, *Bruce Campbell*, who made is claim to fame with a series of low-budget horror films. Bruce wrote a best-selling book titled, *If Chins Could Kill: Confessions of a B-Movie Actor,* that inspired me to write my own book. I highly recommend it.

Street Soldiers did exceptionally well for Jun as he was the executive producer and put some of his own money into the film. Lee not only directed the film, but he was also the writer and editor; it was really his film. Lee graduated from film school, and in 1976, his thesis film, *Button, Button,* won the *Student Academy Award,* which was presented to him by non other than *Steven Spielberg.* Lee wrote, directed, and edited a few other feature films, like the Christmas/Horror film *Silent Night Deadly Night Part 2,* where the killer was a demented Santa Claus. Although it was a low-budget independent film it has since reached cult status and set the tone for every other Christmas slasher film since. The current very successful horror franchise of *Terrifier* films is centered around a demented Santa Claus. Nice try; Lee did it first.

A few years ago, I met a guy at a party. He looked like a Leprechaun. He was short, about 5'3, and had red hair and a beard. I joked and said, hey, weren't you in *Leprechaun 5*? He laughed. We instantly hit it off and joked about making a funny faux Leprechaun trailer. One of us mentioned the *Sharknado* films produced by *The Asylum*, the production company that made millions from the Sharknado franchise. We thought, wouldn't it be funny if we crossed the Sharknado franchise with the *Leprechaun* franchise? And so we did. It was a faux trailer for a movie called *Sharknado vs Leprechaun*.

I sat down and wrote it, and the next week we shot it. Bing. Bang. Boom. I used some of the stock footage from one of the *Sharknado* movies. We shot the scenes against the green screen in my Living Room so we could put whatever background we wanted: a Space Station, an Irish Pub, the White House, etc. It looked great and only cost us a nickel. I cut it together, and it was pretty good, but it wasn't quite what I wanted. I'm not a professional editor and don't have the music, sound effects, and everything else that it really needed. So I gave it to Lee Harry, the Master.

I told Lee I needed some help and he said, "let me tinker around with it." Lee recorded the voiceover, added some dramatic music and sound effects used in that kind of action/horror film. He nailed it; it's a really funny movie trailer spoof. You can watch it on YouTube, *Sharknado vs Leprechaun*. It was very cool of Lee to do that for me. Lee also edited the comedy feature film *Bad President*, starring comedian *Eddie Griffin* and I.

(L to R) *Jason Hwang* **(as Tok), Jeff and** *Jun Chong*

Chapter 24

Tornado Run

Early in my career, I worked with a manager named *Shane White*. He was passionate about what he did, was upfront about everything, and worked hard to get us work. I had many more credits than most of his other clients, so he worked harder for me. He wasn't very well connected, but he did get me out, and we hoped for the best. After all, if he got me one good commercial, a soap opera contract, or a television series, we both could make tens to hundreds of thousands of dollars. Of course, that's everyone's dream in Hollywood: to get that one job that will catapult you to stardom and financial success.

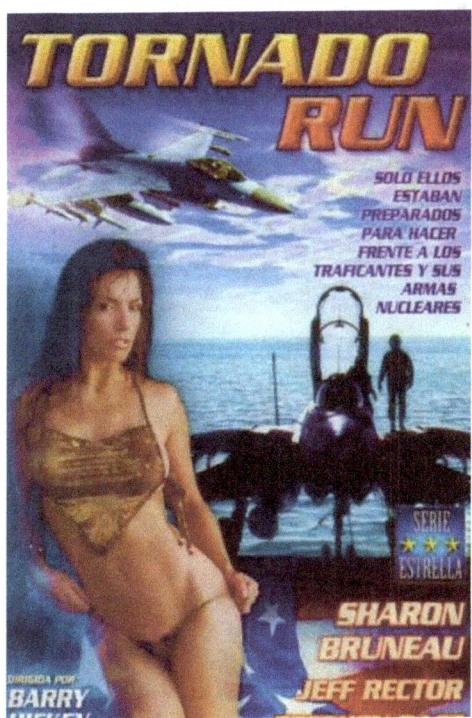

Sharon Bruneau **1991 North America Body Building Champion**

I had been with Shane for about a year when he gathered all his clients for a big announcement. We all assumed he was quitting and throwing in the towel. He started by saying that we were all terrific clients, that he enjoyed working with us (uh, oh, here we go), and that he's decided to close his management company (whoop, there it was). But then, he surprised us by saying that he would now be moving into the production arena and start producing movies of his own and that he wanted us to be in them.

Huh? I didn't see that coming. He then said he had a writer/director friend named *Ulli Lommel* who had access to some money to make a low-budget action/adventure feature film. Since *Top Gun* was a hit at the box office, Shane and Uli decided to make a war film about jet fighter pilots on a mission to rescue some Air Force pilots who had been shot down behind enemy lines. Does the plot sound familiar? It should; it was a mash-up of about five or six popular Top Gun-type films already made at the time. If you can't beat 'em in Hollywood, join 'em by making another similar war film with fighter planes. That film would become *Tornado Run*.

Tornado Run was made on a shoestring budget, but made a lot of money in the foreign market because it was similar to Top Gun, and all the foreign buyers went for it. The trick at the time was using a lot of stock footage[7] in a film, cutting production costs. Smaller films with relatively small budgets could look like bigger-budgeted films using stock footage.

Final version of the movie poster

In this case, they used stock footage of fighter planes flying around and shooting at each other; then they'd cut to a close-up of me in a plane mock-up saying lines like, "He's on my tail!" or "I've got him in my sights, lock, and load!". Then they cut to a close-up

---

7 Stock footage is film footage that has already been shot and used by another production for another film but is repurposed for an entirely different movie.

of my hand on the control stick like I was flying the plane or a close-up of my hand pressing the FIRING button and then cutting to stock footage of a fighter plane firing and blowing up the enemy plane. I would star in many of these types of films that rely heavily on stock footage. When edited together, they look great!

Jeff discovers a traitor

As I mentioned, Tornado Run was very successful. Since it was made for practically nothing (around $40,000), the $300,000 - $400,000 it made was mainly profit. Unfortunately, none of the actors saw the money we were all promised. When the film finished shooting, our "Manager" didn't pay any of us and kept making excuses that he was waiting to get paid by the distributor even though we had signed contracts guaranteeing each of us our salary depending on each of our roles.

Since I was the star of the film, my salary was the largest. But Shane made one big mistake: he set a specific payment date when we were guaranteed to get paid in the contract. Nobody was usually stupid enough to do this, but Shane was inexperienced as a producer. So all the actors got together and took him to court to get our money. The court date arrived, and about eight of us were all on one side of the courtroom, and Shane was alone on the other side.

One by one, we got up and told the judge the same story: Shane was our talent manager; he cast us in the movie, gave us a signed contract, and then reneged on our payment and pocketed all the money. The judge couldn't believe what he was hearing. When it came time for Shane to speak, the judge let him have it. He not only misrepresented himself as a manager but also as the producer of the film. It was an open-and-shut case. The judge ordered Shane to pay us what was owed, and he got off easy as the judge didn't add any additional fees or penalties. When the judge ordered Shane to pay us the thousands of dollars he owed us, Shane White actually turned white as a ghost. We were ecstatic! So, the judge gave us the judgment to take to the court clerk to file against Shane to receive payment.

Jeff and Sharon save the world

Now, here is where the story gets interesting. Eight of us are standing in line to file our judgment, and behind me is another guy in line. He says, "why are you guys so happy?" I said, "We just got a judgment against our manager for screwing us out of some money on a film we all worked on." The man said, "Congratulations!" I said "Thanks." He then said, "So how are you going to collect the money?" I said, "What do you mean?" He said, "You have a judgment against your manager, but how will you make sure he pays you?" I said, "He has to, correct?" He said, "Legally, yes, but if he doesn't pay you, you have to go after him for the money." Huh? "Oh yeah, otherwise, you'll never see a penny." I said, "How do you know all this?" He said. "Because that's what I do. I find out where someone is keeping all their money if they try to hide it to keep from paying off their judgment."

I wasn't sure whether to believe him or not. He then said "You look like you don't believe me." I laugh and say, "That's exactly what I was thinking. He then hands me his business card and says, "Look, here's my card; if you need my help, let me know." So we're

209

all standing outside the courthouse laughing and patting ourselves on the back for our big win in court. One of the other actors asked what I was talking to the guy in line about. I told everyone what he told me, that just because we had a judgment against Shane didn't mean he was ever going to make good on it. Yeah right. Ha! We all had another big laugh about it and went our separate ways. We would not be laughing about it for long.

Sure enough. Shane never paid us a dime, and every time one of us called him to collect, he'd say, oh, I don't have the money, or I got screwed by the distributor, or I'm going to pay you; I promise. It was pretty clear that Shane had no intention of paying us, and he knew that we didn't have the money to go back to court to get it. Now, we're really pissed off, especially since we found out that Shane had just bought himself a brand-new Jeep Cherokee. I don't have any money. Bullshit! So I dug up the guy's business card that he gave me in the courthouse. He answered the phone, and I reminded him of our conversation. He remembered me and asked if we had gotten our money; I said I wouldn't be calling you right now if we had. He said, yeah, that's what I figured.

So we had a long conversation, and I discovered this guy was the real deal. He would go after Shane to find out his bank accounts, property, and assets and where he might be trying to hide his money. The best news was that he didn't want any money upfront; he would only take a percentage of what he collected. I called all the other actors and told them what he said. They were all in! Now, the fun started. Shane had no idea that we had the Terminator on our side and that he was coming for him. So, after our guy does some digging, he finds out that Shane has a bunch of money in several different banks and several assets, including his house, his new Jeep Cherokee, and his wife's Mercedes Benz.

We then find out that he put the Jeep in his wife's name so that we couldn't go after it legally because the judgment was against him not his wife. Shane was a lot of things, but he was no dummy. What we could go after, though, was the Mercedes he had in his name. So we did. Mike filed some papers with the Sheriff's Department to confiscate and sell the car to satisfy the judgment for the money he owed us. Can we do that? I asked, and Mike said, absolutely, it's your right under the law. I said, okay, let's do it. We gave Shane plenty of time to make good on his debt, and he didn't. Now, the kid gloves were coming off.

The next day, an LA County Sheriff showed up at Shane's house with a tow truck. Shane saw this and came out of the house; "What are you doing?" he said; the Sheriff said "I'm confiscating your vehicle to satisfy a court-ordered judgment against you." Shane said "you can't do this" the Sheriff said, "I'm doing it." So his Mercedes got towed away to a storage impound yard. Miraculously, Shane called me up, wanting to make nice. "You should have paid us when we asked; you've forced our hand." "So what are you going to do?" "First, we'll auction off your Mercedes, and that money will be used to pay off as many people as possible. If that isn't enough money, we'll come after more of your assets until everyone is paid. You should have done the right thing in the first place, Shane. We all loved you, we helped you make a profitable film, and then you fucked us!"

Since I was the film star and owed the most money, I was legally in the first position to get any money due. Shane's Mercedes was sold at a car auction, and I was paid what I was owed. The justice system works, folks! Then, the following actors next in line were also paid, but there wasn't enough money in the car sale to pay off everyone. I'm not sure what happened after that, but I believe they went after more of Shane's assets. I got my money, so I moved on.

My twin brother Jerry worked a couple of days on the film since they needed me for some pickup shots, but I was unavailable as I was already shooting a horror film for Lionsgate called *The Darkening*, which was later released as *The Black Gate*. They used him to play me and finish the film. Nobody ever knew that Jerry replaced me in several scenes in the movie. The funniest part of this whole story is that when they auctioned off Shane's Mercedes to pay me, Jerry is the person who bought it at auction for pennies on the dollar. I got my money, and Jerry owned and drove Shane's Mercedes. Welcome to Hollywood!

After the Shane debacle, I wasn't interested in working with any more managers. Still, one day, one of my acting buddies said that he'd found an excellent manager named *Hazel Shallon* and that her company was *Shallon Star Management*. I laughed and said you're kidding, right? *Shallon Star Management*? I laughed again and asked, when's the last time Hazel got you an audition? He said that he went on two today alone. What? I was incredulous. So I asked, "But they were just crappy little, bullshit auditions, right?" He said, "Nope, one was for a network show, and the other was for a national commercial."

He had my attention. Well, what's Hazel like? He said she was cool and that she gets it. She's extremely professional and a hard worker, demanding the same from her clients. My friend was African American and said she was looking for more clients, so he was telling me about her. His name was David, and he was not only an excellent actor but also had a really high booking rate, meaning he booked many jobs on very few auditions. David didn't tell me, and I didn't find out until much later that he and Hazel were sleeping together. No wonder she was so focused on his career. Anyway, I asked for a meeting, he put us together, and the next thing I knew, I had a manager, Hazel, at *Shallon Star Management*, "Where everyone is treated like a star!" Hazel was indeed a great manager; she had a concise list of working actors, so she would guarantee that she would work hard for all of them. I immediately booked a few jobs, including the lead in a skydiving/action film called *A Handful of Wind*.

Jeff with *Steven Pace* as *Captain "Jazz' Wilson*

Chapter 25

A Handful of Wind

Diving into a role

Actor reaches for "Handful of Wind" D

Star dives into high flying adventure film 'A Hand Full of Wind'

Actor Jeff Rector drops to the grou

SHANNON QUINN / The Californian

As an actor, Jeff Rector is willing to go to great lengths for his craft. He's dived the deep sea, skied down mountainsides and tested his martial arts mettle with Jean Claude Van Damme in Hong Kong.

This week, his dedication reached new heights. With only a day of training, he jumped out of an airplane at 2,500 feet to prepare for his role in the film "A Hand Full of Wind."

Parachuting over Perris, Rector performed one jump after another in an effort to earn his sky diving certificate in time to do his own stunts for the film.

"I got to fly like a bird and lived to tell about it!" Rector said. "I always wanted to sky dive."

Rector was attracted to the role of the renegade Air Force paratrooper Harlee because of the film's strong script and his desire to add a new skill to his repertoire.

"I have a chance to do something I've never done before and for an actor, that's very exciting," he said.

With a resume that reads like an advertisement for an action-adventure hero, there's little Rector hasn't done. The actor, stuntman and stand-up comedian has the versatility to ski, dive, shoot and sing. A martial arts expert, Rector and his twin brother Jerry earned co-star status alongside Jean Claude Van Damme in "Double Impact."

"I do my own stunts for my movies," Rector said. "It's more realistic for an actor to do his own stunts. Then there's no break in the action."

Still, Rector admits he experienced a moment of hesitation when it came to taking the leap of faith.

"When I got to the plane door at 12,500 feet and felt the wind blowing in my face and saw how far the ground is below, I had second thoughts," he said, with a grin. "But you just suck it up and you go."

Producer Frank Evans worked with Rector on other projects and said he had faith in the actor's ability to handle the physically demanding role.

Filming for the high-flying adventure will take place over the next 2-3 weeks around and above the Perris Airport. Other locations include the Perris City Hall, various Sun City homes and Defazio's Saloon and Dance Hall in Winchester. Owned by a family in Temecula, the restaurant will be re-named "O Chute" for the film. The proprietor of the establishment will be Patsy Swayze, who joins her sons Don and Patrick in the project.

Don Swayze has a starring role in the film. Patrick Swayze will appear in a supporting role as a member of an opposing sky diving team. Also featured are actresses Marcia Swayze ("Dark Secrets") and Ellen Wheeler ("Another World" "St. Elsewhere"); and national sky diving teams from the U.S.,

Canada and Japan.

Rector plays the good guy, an ex-Air Force paratrooper, who the actor calls "a rebel without a chute."

"He gets a letter from a friend who's a sky diver asking him to come. He leaves the Air Force and goes to see his buddy who's part of a jump team out here. When he gets here he finds out his friend died two weeks before. His chute didn't open and he got into some real estate. He bought the farm, so to speak," the actor said with a wry smile.

Suspecting foul play, Rector's character joins the jump team to investigate.

Directed by Oscar-winner John Buschelman, "A Hand Full of Wind," from Film Street Production, Inc., is scheduled for release through Tri-Star pictures in mid-October.

Flanked by instructors Philip Stapleton (left) and Steve Clark (right), actor Jeff Rector returns to the flight school after his second jump. JOHN GEORGE / The Californ

Jeff Rector, takes off his chute with the assistance of flight instructor Steve Clark.

Local newspaper article publicising the film

I'm going to share with you a story I haven't told many people. *I almost died in a skydiving accident.* It's true, and here are the crazy circumstances that led up to that particular death-defying moment in my life. I would never tell anyone who wanted to experience skydiving not to do it. It is an incredible thrill and very safe to jump

in tandem with an instructor who ultimately controls the jump. Just make sure you're willing to jump out of a perfectly good airplane at 10,000 feet above the Earth to do it.

At this point in my career, I was on a roll, starring in a slew of independent films and TV shows that included horror, suspense, action, romance, and comedy. Some of those stories will follow this up in later chapters. The only thing I hadn't done was a western; I thought riding a horse and shooting a gun at the same time would be cool. For my next film, I was cast as the lead in a skydiving movie called *A Handful of Wind*. I played the role of Harley, an Airborne Army Ranger for the military. These guys are the Navy Seals of skydiving. They're trained to jump from high altitudes, even at night, and infiltrate the enemy behind their lines and in the most dangerous situations. They are, quite frankly, the best of the best.

Harley received a letter from his best friend (another Ranger), who was discharged from the service several months earlier. He was the leader of a competitive skydiving team and wanted Harley to be part of the team when he, too, would be discharged in a few weeks. My character was named Harley because he rode a Harley-Davidson motorcycle (original, huh?) and arrived home weeks later to reunite with his buddy.

Harley found out immediately that his friend had recently died in a skydiving accident when his Parachute failed to open. Not believing that someone as trained as a Ranger would make such a simple mistake, he joined the Skydiving Team to get to the bottom of things. Harley soon discovered that someone had deliberately tampered with his friend's Parachute, causing him to be killed. As the movie played out, Harley finds the killer's identity and gets his revenge. Whoops, spoiler alert! I was very excited to play this part and to be able to skydive, which was always on my bucket list. I'm very athletic and always wanted to try it one day.

I usually do as many of my stunts as possible for filming (martial arts, stage combat, guns, weaponry, etc.) I can do some high falls if necessary, but I'm not going through a plate-glass window; that's what the real stunt guys are for. The production company put me through a series of skydiving lessons to be certified to do my own jumps and landings to make it more realistic. I was thrilled at the opportunity.

We were shooting out at the Perris Airfield, about an hour and a half east of Los Angeles, on the way toward Palm Springs.

To be certified, you must make ten individual jumps from an aircraft. My first jump was Tandem, which meant you're strapped to an instructor, jumping and landing together. The instructor does all the work, and you're just along for the ride. When people tell you they went skydiving for the first time, they usually talk about a tandem jump.

Here's what happens: your instructor puts on a parachute, and you both board a small twin-engine airplane that takes you up to about 10,000 feet. You both jump out of the plane, and your instructor pulls the rip chord. The Parachute opens, and you float back down to Earth. The instructor pulls on the two parachute control straps about ten feet above the ground, dramatically slowing down your descent. If you pull too soon, you can have a very hard landing. If you pull them too late, you can break both of your legs. Timing is very crucial when landing from such a high altitude.

As we were ascending to the correct altitude, I could smell

the fuel and oil from the plane's prop engines; it was not a pretty smell. It also added uneasiness to the experience. We were all sitting facing each other on bench seats on either side of the plane (no first-class recliners here). As we reached the jump altitude, they opened up the back door of the airplane. We're all used to flying and looking out the window to see square patches of land on the ground from high up. But when they opened that door, and there was nothing but open air and the ground below, a sudden feeling of dread washed over me. Maybe this wasn't such a great idea.

The instructor and I walked over to the very edge of the open door. He said, "We're going on three, one, two." On two he hurled us both out of the plane. No getting cold feet now; we were plummeting toward Earth. Wow, what a rush! Suddenly, I was flying through the air. Superman had nothing on us. After about a minute, the instructor pulled the rip chord, and our beautiful white chute opened. As we floated down, the 360-degree view from that altitude

Jeff (left) in freefall for his skydiving certification

was amazing; it was exactly how I imagined it would be.

I wanted a video to document this, so I paid one of their videographers to shoot us. They have a video camera mounted to their helmet and jump out of the plane ahead of you to videotape you exiting the plane, all the action of your jump, and even your landing. I was amazed at the video footage's clarity when I finally saw it. It was well worth the $40 I paid to have the experience documented and to make all of my friends jealous.

Okay, let's jump ahead (pun intended). I had already completed my 4th jump and was on the way to being certified. Until that point, I had two instructors on either side of me to ensure I did everything correctly. There aren't many second chances in skydiving. If you screw up, you can easily die; if you do everything right and land wrong, you can still break your legs. It's definitely not a sport for the squeamish.

This was my first "solo" jump, it was just me and my instructor, who would be right in front of me, giving me the hand signals to complete this portion of the jump. First, I had to turn my body around 360 degrees to the left (which I did). Then I had to turn my around 360 degrees to the right (which I did). Then I had to do a complete back flip in the air and return back to my starting position (which I did perfectly). Woo Hoo! I did it!

My instructor gave me the thumbs up; I looked around and signaled with my arms so that any jumper around us knew I was about to open my Parachute. It's a weird sensation when you open a parachute for the first time; it feels like you're getting yanked straight up into the sky. But the reality is, it stops your descent so fast that it feels as though you're going upward, but you're not. Note: the production paid a videographer for every one of my jumps in order to document my progress.

I signaled and grabbed for the ripcord, but in my haste, I didn't pull the ripcord hard enough and it didn't completely deploy. The very Parachute that was supposed to get me to the ground in one piece had not deployed and I'm still falling from the sky. The instructor immediately looked at me like, "What the fuck are doing?" I looked at him like, "What the Fuck am I doing?" Then the cameraman who was still recording looked at me like, "What the fuck are you doing? I'm out of here!" The cameraman flew off and opened his Parachute. I guess he didn't think it was a good idea to videotape me hitting the ground. There isn't much time to think as you plummet towards the ground at a hundred feet per second.

There's an expression in skydiving when your parachute malfunctions and you hit the ground. They say, "You're getting into Real Estate" (literally). The training teaches you that if there is ever a problem with your Parachute and you have to release it, you immediately reach for your reserve parachute, which I did. The reserve chute opened beautifully, except for the fact that I hadn't completely released my main chute, and if the two got tangled up, I'd be getting into some real estate real quick. The instructor shouted, "Cut away your main chute." I immediately grabbed the ripcord again and was able to release my main Parachute.

Hooray, I wasn't going to die. At least not yet. I saw my instructor's parachute below me since he pulled his ripcord much earlier. A car almost hit him as he dropped out of the sky onto the road below. If you delay pulling your ripcord too long, you get too close to the ground for your Parachute to do much good. I was dangerously close to that altitude, but the good news was I had a beautiful open parachute, which slowed my descent, but I was all on my own at this point.

Jeff safely comes in for a landing

The good news was that my Parachute opened; the bad news was that I was no longer over the drop zone, and I was looking at rooftops and power lines, trying to figure out whose swimming I was going to land in. I looked ahead and saw some railroad tracks that ran between the housing projects. I swung around and was able to land next to the railroad tracks, but the ground was extremely uneven and sloped downward, a far cry from the flat landing zone of the tarmac that I was used to. If I misjudged my landing, I could (you guessed it) break my legs. Halfway down, I started reciting the Lord's Prayer and prayed that he would save me.

Miraculously, I landed perfectly, got down on my knees, and kissed the ground. The videographer alerted the ground crew, who sent a truck out to pick up me and my instructor. We were now about 2 miles south of the drop zone. They picked us up in the airfield utility truck. I must have been white as a ghost, sitting in the back of the pickup with my Parachute tucked between my legs. I don't remember my instructor's name, but he was one of these extreme sports guys who surfed, skydived, base jumped, and everything else dangerous. He was ecstatic about what had just transpired.

Instructor: "WOO HOO! Dude! You did it! You saved yourself! Whoa, what a rush, huh? Me: (sarcastically) Yeah, what a rush! Well, I guess that's it for today, huh? Instructor: Hell no, let's go back up? Go back up? I felt like throwing up. I wanted to get in my car and drive back to LA as fast as I could. I also knew that if I left, I would never be able to jump again, and I still had a skydiving film to shoot. So, against all odds, I decided to go back up and do it right. Me: Sure, let's go! I have to tell you that I have never been more frightened in my life. I was shaking as the plane climbed back up to our jumping altitude. I could once again smell the gas and oil mixture from the prop engines, which almost made me nauseous. I prayed once again. They opened the door, and we jumped out. I performed the dive flawlessly and remembered pulling the right cord this time. The jump couldn't have been any more textbook.

I have never been more scared to do something in my entire life. I literally stared Death right in the face and said, "Fuck you death! I will never let fear alone defeat me!" That one jump, that one act of defiance (stupidity), made me fearless; to this day, nothing scares me anymore. If only I had the videotape of that experience, it would have been something.

Jeff is safe and sound on the ground

When the Producers found out what had happened and that I went back up to jump again, they were furious. For insurance reasons, if their star had died skydiving that would have been the end of the movie and the bad press would have sealed the fate of the film. There was a huge wave of relief from everyone, including me when I landed safely from the second jump. The Producers said that they preferred I wait until all the principal filming was finished on the ground before I finished my skydiving certification. That sounded good to me. I agreed, and two days later, we started principal photography on *A Handful of Wind*. Compared to my skydiving incident, the shooting was a real breeze.

The filming schedule called for all the action on the ground to be filmed first, and the more difficult aerial and skydiving sequences would be filmed second. Since we were all supposed to be part of an elite skydiving team, the production company hired some of the best skydivers around who would stunt double us for all the tricky skydiving maneuvers. At that time, no one had ever shot a dramatic skydiving film before, and with all the experts doubling us, they were going to shoot some exciting and never-before-seen aerial footage. We were all very excited to be part of it.

The film was directed by *Stephen Furst*, who played *Flounder* in the classic comedy *Animal House* starring *John Belushi*. I had worked with Stephen on another film, *Magic Kid II*. We had a great cast of mostly unknown actors because of the limited budget. I was the lead hero; the lead bad guy was played by *Deke Anderson*, a great actor who I worked with before on a martial arts/action film, *Ballistic*. Deke also doubled *Bruce Campbell* along with my brother Jerry on the *Sam Raimi* film *Army of Darkness*. The leading lady played my girlfriend; she was relatively new but very talented. We had a light love scene in the movie, and she was nervous because she had never kissed another actor on screen before. We spent the afternoon getting to know each other, and I suggested that we practice kissing so that it wouldn't be so awkward on the set. She agreed, and since neither of us was involved with anyone at the time, we wound up together during and after we wrapped production.

She was very sweet, and we had great chemistry. The love scene was so hot that the entire crew went outside to smoke a cigarette afterward.

We wrapped the film's first part on time and had a party with the cast, crew, and local skydivers. Everyone was in great spirits and excited about the upcoming aerial shoot. I was ready to continue my certification and felt really good about going back up and jumping again. I was featured in several local newspapers and asked to be the Grand Marshall in the Perris Fourth of July celebration. In the parade, I rode in the back of a convertible Cadillac and waved to the locals. I was treated as though I was an astronaut who had just returned from a trip to the moon.

I lived on location in Perris for the entire shoot. Since I was the lead, I didn't have many days off. Production cut everyone's paychecks every Friday, and we deposited them on Saturday or Monday. Because I needed some cash for the weekend, I went to the bank the next day. I saw one of the other actors just ahead of me in line. He cashed his check and left. When I got to the bank teller, my check bounced. I said, what's going on? The teller said there wasn't enough money in the account to cash my check.

I said that's ridiculous; we're shooting a film, and that check is from the production company. I just saw one of the other actors cash his check two minutes ago. She said, that's right, there was enough money for his check. I was livid; I went the producer's hotel room. What's going on? They said they had gone over budget but expected to get some cash from the investors, not to worry. They said to head back to LA, and they'd let me know in a week or so when we would go back into production.

But they never did. The film was never finished, the skydiving sequences were never shot, and the producers were unceremoniously run out of town. They owed a lot of people a lot of money. Because they liked me and I was involved from the inception, they wound up paying me everything they owed. Most of the other actors, including the director, were not so fortunate. The irony was that after almost killing myself taking skydiving lessons, none of the aerial skydiving scenes were ever shot. That was the second time I almost died on location shooting a film that never saw the light of day.

Chapter 26

Hellmaster

After the dissapointing experience of *A Handful of Wind* I got cast in a horror film that would be shot in Detroit, Michigan. Fantastic! The film was going to be called *Them*. But when the movie

was released, the distributor would change the title to *Hellmaster*, which I liked better anyway. I asked my agent what part of Detroit we were shooting in. He said a city called Pontiac. Pontiac? I said, I grew up in Pontiac! Woo hoo! My agent wasn't quite as thrilled as I was. I'm going to film in my hometown, where many of my old buddies, including *Fritz Webber*, still lived, so it would also be a homecoming reunion. The production company flew me to Detroit and put me in a nearby hotel. I decided to come in a few days early and have a little reunion party with my childhood chums. We partied that night, and I regaled them with my stories of Hollywood stardom. Even though many of my films were low-budget independents, it didn't matter; I was still a bonafide movie star.

I met with the director and producer the next day to review the shooting schedule and what was expected for my role. There was an issue with the actor they had already cast in the larger role as the main antagonist. I didn't know what the issue was, but I didn't ask. So the director, *Douglas Schultz*, said he wanted me to play the bigger part as this bad boy college student with a hard edge, an attitude and who carried around a bullwhip. I know, cool, right? Things couldn't be better; I was getting paid to be back home and on vacation with my friends for a few weeks.

Already, things were going great, I was not only back home with my pals for a few weeks, but I was now one of the leads in this new horror film. I also found out that the lead psycho killer would be played by the famous actor *John Saxon*, whom I knew from the *Bruce Lee* film *Enter the Dragon* and a number of TV shows and movies. He also played the Sheriff in the iconic *Nightmare on Elm Street* films. I then found out that another recognizable actor had also been cast. His name was *David Emge*, and he starred in the *George Romero* zombie classic, *Dawn of the Dead*. David

John Saxon

was a great guy and very down-to-earth. Dawn of the Dead was one of my favorite genre films at the time.

We started shooting; the film took place in a university 20 years after a horrific accident that killed a number of students. Part of the movie would take place in the Universities creepy basement laboratory where a nutty professor created a serum that mutated its

Eric Kingston **about to take another victim**

subjects into gory killers.

One of the actors who gets injected with this serum was *Eric Kingston*. It turned out that Eric was a martial arts expert and specialized in a variety of weapons. In *Hellmaster*, he had this nightstick with a little sickle on the end that he would spin around and impale me with. Why? Because it's a horror movie, and people get killed in horror films, especially in a variety of bloody, gory, and horrific ways. I knew what I signed up for.

A not so nice mutant Catholic school girl

Another one of the actors was *Ron Asheton*. He was a famous local musician who played in a band called *The Psychedelic Stooges* or *Iggy Pop and The Stooges*. Singer *Iggy Pop* originally formed the band in Ann Arbor, Michigan.

In the film, Ron played a psychotic nun who also gets injected with the serum and turns into a murderous, mutated psychopath.

I really don't remember much about the production, except that everyone was really nice and it was great to see my childhood friends again. Eric Kingston eventually moved to Hollywood years later to pursue his career as an actor. We reunited and are still good friends to this day. Hellmaster received a great write-up and four-page spread in *Fangoria* magazine, the number-one Horror magazine in the world. The director, *Douglas Schultz*, has since made several horror films and opened up one of Michigan's most successful film training schools. I'm happy for him. .

A hapless female driver is about to be the next contestant on "Syringe Along With Mitch."

One of *Soulstealer's* ghouls succumbs to the worst kind of overdose.

John Paxon takes a cue from his old nemesis, Freddy Krueger, in Dealing with Joel (Sean Sweeney).

had all these bodyguards around him and I wasn't allowed to talk to him, but Roseanne was great. She joked with us a lot."

Detroit, White insists, is a great place to work in the film business. "People ask me, 'Is it hard doing all this stuff out here in Michigan, away from Los Angeles and all the technology?' And I tell them no. Detroit, believe it or not, is one of the major film centers in the country. Many of the best commercial and industrial films are made right here. We have everything we need, including soundstages, stuff for animation, makeup and effects."

There are four major monsters in *Soulstealer*, Schulze provided White with background notes on each, and a few words on his makeup philosophy. "I told him that I wanted the prosthetics to be skin-tight," comments Schulze. "I wanted them to look like actual faces, to look real. So many of the creature masks in today's films look like they run from the shoulder up, like they're not really a part of the body. Or they're way too big in proportion. On this film, I wanted realism."

The result is a cross between Barker's *Nightbreed* creations and Romero's zombies. The first of the lead ghouls is called Razor-face, because after getting an injection, he finds out that he likes to cut his face up with razors." White describes. Creature number two is the Monkey-Boy. "The role was played by a 12-year-old in makeup." White continues. "He looks like he's 60 years old, and in

continued on page 77)

Chapter 27

Marching Out of Time

After Hellmaster I was back in L.A. when I noticed an ad in *Backstage,* an industry casting magazine, for an "untitled" science-fiction/action/comedy with time-traveling Nazis that was looking for a handsome actor to play a police officer. I'm in! So, I submitted my headshot and resume to the production and got an audition. I booked the lead role as *Lieutenant Butch*, a Los Angeles Police Officer who

Jeff as *Lieutant Butch* the films action hero

was the hero of this action/comedy.

Because I had a very clean-cut, all-American look, I've been cast as a lot of Police Officers, FBI Agents, Sheriffs, Detectives, you name it. One day, I decided to invest in an authentic police uniform, so I went to the local uniform company. I got outfitted with the official LAPD uniform, complete with a badge, belt, gun, name tag, shoes, etc. I looked like a real, authentic LA cop whenever I wore the uniform. I used to love going into an audition; the receptionist would see me and think I was a real cop, and they'd say, uh, hello, officer, can I help you? "Yes, is that your car double-parked on the street?" "Oh, no, sir," and then they'd remember that they are casting for a cop role, and they'd say, "you're not a real cop, are you?" "Nope," and I'd walk back to the casting office. Ha! Fooled another one!

One time, I was wearing my police uniform and left an audition. I drove home from Beverly Hills around noon and was hungry. I passed an Indian restaurant and chicken curry sounded pretty good at the time. I parked, went in and was seated. I order my food, ate, and went to the register to pay for lunch. The owner said lunch was on them for all the excellent work I do. Huh? That's when I realized I was wearing my police uniform, so I said, Oh, uh, right, "To Protect and Serve"! (which is the LAPD motto). I thanked them for a delicious lunch and left before they realized I wasn't a real cop. I still wonder if they noticed me climbing into a Nissan sedan, not a black-and-white police cruiser. Thinking back, I should have still paid the bill, but then, I wouldn't have that great story for my book. God only knows how much bad Karma I got for that one.

Marching Out of Time was a time-traveling comedy. The story and plot were simple. A nebbish neighbor named *Fred Johnson* hears strange noises coming from the house next door during the Christmas Holiday. Fred's family has left him "Home Alone" to finish some work before he meets up with them later. When he knocks on the neighbor's door to investigate, nobody answers. He spies on the house with binoculars to see who's coming and

He's not just home alone, he's saving the world.

MARCHING OUT OF TIME

going and is astonished to see World War II Nazi soldiers going in and out, and so he calls the police. I show up, hear his complaint, write a report, and leave because no one is answering the door, and I don't believe that there are German soldiers from the second World War running around. I'm called back to his house a second and third time, and I'm just about to arrest him for filing a false complaint when I see the Germans, too. I exclaim, "Oh my God, there are Nazis next door!" "That's what I've been trying to tell you." Fred says.

Fred's neighbor, Professor Memo (*Matthew Hennerson*), is a wacky scientist that creates a teleportation chamber that converges with a German version and accidentally teleports Nazi soldiers from 1942 Germany to 1992 Palmdale, California, fifty years into the Future. They take over Memo's house, and for the rest of the movie, Fred and I try to figure out how to thwart this SoCal Nazi invasion, and comedy ensues. When the Germans realize we are onto their plan to change history, they jump through the time portal back to 1942. Fred and I follow them back in time, realizing that we have to destroy the time machine in the past to save the future. Sound familiar? Basically, every time travel plot ever written.

Jeff and Fred discover Nazis next door

Fred was played by a relatively new actor named *Frederick Anderson.* Fred was hilarious in the role, and we had great chemistry as it was a buddy film of sorts, the nebbish, reluctant neighbor, and the strong, confident by-the-book police officer. I played the role straight, and Fred played the role for the laughs. I was *Dean Martin*, and Fred was *Jerry Lewis.* We played off each other great; the movie received favorable reviews from the critics and made a lot of money.

It was a lot of fun; I did all of my own stunts, including hand-to-hand combat with several of the German soldiers. It was quite gratifying kicking Nazis in the teeth! We shot the movie in a neighborhood in Palmdale that was still under construction, so all of the homes were empty. It was perfect; we could shoot guns and make as much noise as we wanted to including crash a car and there were no neighbors around to complain about it. We literally had our own private street location for the shoot.

While taking a break from filming one day and I was sitting next to the writer and director, *Antone Vasil*, while they were setting up the next shot. I asked him how many guys he had read for my role. About fifty, he said. Why did you pick me? The director laughed and said, "When you walked into the audition in your police uniform, I said, that's the Guy! Also, I didn't have to spend any money renting you a uniform." "Oh," I said, "good to know!" Then he said, "But you really were the best actor out of everyone; the uniform was just a bonus." Since then, that uniform has paid for itself twenty times

(L to R) *Jimmy Boveen*, *Robert Z'Dar* **and** *Heinrich James*

over. Clothing really does make the man.

The film also starred *Robert Z'Dar*, who played the Nazi scientist, Muck, who created the Nazi version of the teleporter. Robert was best known for the cult horror film franchise, *Maniac Cop I & II*. He was also in *Tango and Cash* with *Kurt Russell* and *Sylvester Stallone*. Z'Dar was known for his fascinating appearance due to his cherubism, a medical condition resulting in an enlarged jawline. Z'dar had a unique and easily recognizable face that appeared slightly sinister, which aided his career as he usually portrayed villains. I've done several films with Robert over the years, and we were good friends until his passing in 2015 from congestive heart failure.

Another one of the Nazis, *Colonel Von Kontz*, was played by *Heinrich James*. Heinrich was also in the big-budget Disney action/adventure film *The Rocketeer*, starring *Bill Campbell, Jennifer Connolly*, and *Alan Arkin*. *The Rocketeer* is still one of my favorite films. It was ground-breaking at the time, and the director, *Joe Johnson*, went on to direct *Captain America: The First Avenger* for *Marvel Entertainment*. Heinrich's famous line in The Rocketeer was in the big finale fight scene in a Nazi Airship; Heinrich threateningly says to *Timothy Dalton*, "You Actor!" and Dalton promptly shoves him out the door of the dirigible to fall thousands of feet to his death. A few years before, Bill and I performed Shakespeare in the Park as part of the Southern California Renaissance Faire in a production of *Taming of the Shrew*. Bill played the lead, *Petruchio*, and I played the second lead *Lucentio*.

Although *Marching Out of Time* was a comedy, it could have easily been an excellent dramatic thriller. The film's original comedic title was *Back To The Fuhrer*, a spoof on the title of the *Michael J. Fox* comedy hit, *Back To The Future*. The film was set to be released around the same time as *Steven Spielberg's* World War II drama, *Schindler's List*. Artist View Entertainment would distribute the film and change the title to Marching Out of Time.

The story's sci-fi and time portal aspects were well thought out, and the script was excellent.

The film was released in 1993 by *Cinequanon Distribution* in the United States (the same company that released *Tornado Run* and my next film, *Legion of the Night*). The film did incredibly well both here in the US and overseas and sold to many foreign countries. I laughed when *Scott Jones*, President of *Artist View*, said that Germany paid the highest amount for the film and that it was one of the foreign countries that enjoyed it the most.

Chapter 28

Legion of the Night

Several years later, out of the blue, I get a call from *Ron Asheton*, my friend from *Hellmaster*. He said he was co-starring in another horror film in Pontiac, he recommended me to the director (who liked my work in *Hellmaster*) and wanted to hire me for one of the roles. Sweet. Another paid vacation back to Pontiac.

Legion of the Night was about a scientist, (Dr. Bloom) played by *William (Bill) Hinzman*. Bill was *George Romero's* cinematographer on the original zombie classic, *Night of the Living Dead*. The writer/director, *Matt Jaisle*, was a big fan of the film and cast Bill as the mad scientist even though Bill was a cinematographer, not an actor. Surprisingly, Bill was fantastic in the role. I played a Detroit gangster named *Francis Vansemie'* who discovered that the doctor had created a serum that could reanimate dead bodies. Vansemie' had the idea to create a "Legion of the Night," an army of zombie killers known as CZA's (Cybernetic Zombie Assassins) to kill off the other

231

gangs in the city and eliminate his competition. Cool idea, right?

So Vansemie' blackmails Dr. Bloom into creating this CZA "army of the undead" to do his bidding. Everything goes

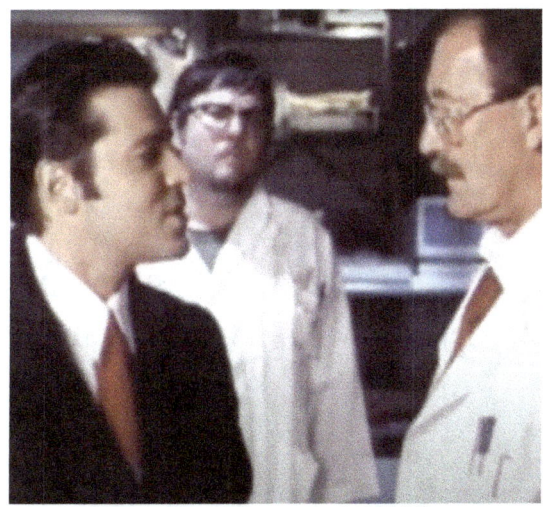

according plan until a malfunction in the CZA's cause them to go berserk and start massacring everything in sight. It was a horror film after all.

I loved the script because it was a great combination of science fiction, action, and horror, my three favorite genres!

Jeff with *Ron Asheton* and *Bill Hinzman*

Also, I got to be the lead bad guy and terrorize everyone in the film. Because I was a "Hollywood actor" and had a lot of credits, the director let me improvise and used just about every idea I came up with to make

my character, the script, and the movie more interesting. I had a ball! The lead hero was a Detroit actor named *Tim Lovelace,* and no, he's not related to the famous porn star *Linda Lovelace.* I asked. Tim was a great guy, and in addition to acting, he was a renowned local hunter and marksman and would get paid big bucks to take guys on expensive weekend hunting trips around Michigan when hunting season started. Tim knew his way with guns, and there were plenty of them in this film! We all had guns: Tim, me, the CZAs, everyone. We went through a lot of ammo. Safely of course.

***Tim Lovelace* ready for action**

I had so much free reign on this movie that I even got a few of my local buddies, *Brad Henson* and my best friend Fritz, cast as drug dealers. In one of the scenes, they were about to make a big drug deal when the CZA's surprised them and took them out.

The director hired a local stripper to play my mob girlfriend. The idea was that during the shootout, one of the CZA's would grab her, pull down her top (revealing her breasts) before strangling her with a chord. It was pretty violent, but that's what the director

Jeff with his Mob girlfriend

wanted. One of the stunt CZA's was instructed to pull down her top and strangle her. Take after take, he just couldn't do it right and was wasting valuable shooting time which we didn't have. So I said to him, give me your wardrobe, which was an all-black Ninja-type jumpsuit with a hoodie, high-tech goggles, and a ventilator-type face mask. All black. The look of the CZA's was really cool.

The stunt guy quickly got out of his costume, handed it to me, and I threw it on. The director yelled action. I shoot the drug dealers, grab the girl, and she screams; I pull down her top, strangle her with a chord. CUT! That was it. Perfect. In one take. I took off the costume, handed it back to the stunt guy, and we kept shooting. There was no time to

233

waste on these independent films. You have to shoot and shoot fast. If you ever get to see *Legion of the Night*, you'll know that's me in the CZA outfit killing the the dealers girlfriend. At the end of the scene the CZA's were shooting at me, so I dove over a railing and flew in slow-motion through the air while shooting at them. I landed on the ground, and kept shooting. That scene was one of my favorites in the entire film and I still use it on my stunt reel.

The production company had rented one of the abandoned areas of the Pontiac Mental Institution for most of the locations. At the time, it was a real, working nut house that was right across the street from the Pontiac Mall, where we all used to hang out as kids. The Institution was made up of a series of large seven-story

Jeff tests the drugs prior to making a deal

buildings on a huge plot of land. We were shooting in one of the abandoned hospital wings, which was all torn up. There was paint peeling off the walls, rusted bed frames with missing mattresses and, old rusted cabinets, making it really creepy and eerie, so it was perfect for a horror film.

One night, we're shooting outside on the grounds, and I noticed this woman in a nightgown who was standing around the set as one of the extras. She was really quiet and kept to herself. Then we broke for dinner. When we came back from our dinner break and were about to start shooting again, two orderlies from the mental Institution come over and grabbed this woman. Turned out she wasn't an extra at all. She was one of the mental patients who had wandered off from the hospital, and they couldn't find her. She made her way over to our set, and the director mistakenly thought she was one of our extras. Why not? She looked great. We can laugh about it now, but you never know how mentally unstable somebody is, and sometimes things like that can go horribly awry.

Ron Asheton uses a CZA as a shield

About halfway through the movie, my character gets killed by Lovelace. What? The main bad guy dies in the middle of the movie? Not so fast. My mob doctors recover my body and take it back to the laboratory, where they use the serum to reanimate my corpse, bringing me back to life. Now, I'm the gangster zombie who goes after Lovelace's character and kills him. His people then bring him back to life as the hero zombie. For the rest of the film, it's good zombie vs bad zombie! It really was a very clever and well-written script. Of course, my character gets killed really violently for a second time at the end of the film (the director liked violence). For my second death, I was lying on the floor after getting shot by

Jeff in a fatal shootout

Lovelace, like twenty times. The director once again wanted to go over the top. He took a gallon jug of fake movie blood and started pouring it all over my body, all over my face, and into my mouth. The director yelled action! I'm covered in blood, choking on it and spitting it out of my mouth; that's as REAL as it gets.

We definitely only needed one take of that one! One thing that all actors can agree on, it's really fun to do a death scene or to be killed in a movie. It's morose, I know, but it's true. In *Legion of the Night,* I got to play two death scenes in one film, an actor's dream! I don't know how many actors can say they did that.

I was on a roll with a series of action and horror films, *Street Soldiers, Marching Out of Time, Hellmaster* and *Legion of the Night* and the trend would continue for my next film, *The Darkening*.

236

Chapter 29

The Darkening aka The Black Gate

The Darkening was a supernatural horror film that took place in a bed and breakfast that sat atop a picturesque cliff overlooking the ocean. I played a psychic investigator, best-selling author, and expert on the supernatural who was summoned when the woman who owned the house began experiencing terrifying supernatural experiences driving her customers away and destroying her business. I'm hired to investigate, discover what's happening, and help the owner eliminate any ghosts, demons, etc., if they do exist. It doesn't take me long to realize that a dark, evil entity does exist in the house. At the movie's end, it turns out that the house was built over the gates of Hell.

William (Bill) Mesa was the director, cinematographer, and visual effects supervisor (VES). Bill Mesa was a visual effects supervisor for a company called *Introvision* that did the effects for some of Hollywood's biggest movies, including the fantastic train crash sequence for *The Fugitive* starring *Harrison*

Ford. *Introvision* was the state-of-the-art visual effects process before CGI (Computer Generated Imagery) was invented. Bill also worked on *Darkman* and the supernatural/action/comedy *Army of Darkness* starring *Bruce Campbell* and directed by a newcomer at the time named *Sam Raimi,* who would also direct the follow-up TV series *Ash Versus the Evil Dead*.

Sam went on to become an A list director of such films as *Spiderman I, II & III, Dr. Strange and the Multiverse of Madness* and many others. Interestingly enough Sam wanted to cast Jerry and I to double *Bruce Campbell* for a specific scene in *Army of Darkness*. I was cast as the lead in a vampire film *Nightfall* and was not available, but Jerry worked on the film and can be seen on the poster.

Sam, Bruce, and Sam's brother, *Ted Raimi*, grew up just a few miles from me in Oak Park, Michigan. We were all making monster movies in the woods with our friends using an 8MM camera (the best there was at the time). But we didn't know each other until many years later when I met Sam and Bruce at a local softball game when they too moved to California for fame and fortune.

Years later, *Ted Raimi* would do a cameo in my first (professional) short film, *Fatal Kiss*, about present-day vampires living in Los Angeles. *Fatal Kiss* starred the beautiful and incredibly sexy *Tane' McClure* ("Legally Blonde" films), veteran actors *James Karen* ("Return of the Living Dead"), *Carel Struyken* (Lurch in the "Addams Family" films), *Kato Kaelin* (O.J. Simpson's housemate) and a cameo by *Forrest J. Ackerman* (his 100th cameo). I wrote, directed, produced, and starred in *Fatal Kiss*, which eventually sold to *HBO*. That's another chapter for my next book.

The screenplay for *The Darkening* was written by famed Novelists and Screenwriters *Victoria Parker* and *John G. Jones*. John is a New York Times best-selling author of many of the *Amityville Horror* novels in the franchise, including *Amityville Horror II, Amityville: The Evil Escapes, Amityville: The Final Chapter*, and *Amityville Horror Christmas*. John and Victoria were longtime friends of Bill's. They brought Bill their original screenplay and asked him to direct it (his directorial debut), which he agreed to.

We shot at a farmhouse in Simi Valley built in the 1800's that was supposedly haunted, which added another air of mystery to the project. In the film I discover an old antique chest with ancient markings on it that had been hidden in the attic. There were some ancient incantations in one of the secret drawers which summoned the evil entity possessing the house. Utilizing his dark power, he tried to destroy me, but I'm the hero and I have God on my side, so I destroy the demon with holy water and the power of the Bible.

The female lead in the film was *Rebecca Kyler Downs*, a beautiful, voluptuous, brunette actress who played the woman who owned the bed and breakfast. Rebecca was an excellent actress, and most of our scenes were together since we were the two stars of the film. She tells me the house's history, the strange things that have been happening, and why she thinks an evil presence inhabits it. Horror films can be unusually emotional for an actor since many scenes have to be scary, intense, and life-threatening in order to sell the horror and danger involved. Horror films are far more emotionally draining for actors than light and fluffy romantic comedies, where you usually get to laugh throughout the production.

Unsurprisingly, actors in a film or TV show can become romantically involved. You're working together for twelve-hour days for two to three months sometimes, and that connection on screen can turn into real romantic feelings, especially with the level of trust that is involved with a particular script. Rebecca and I did a lot of rehearsing together and hit it off. I found her to be quite attractive, sexy, and sweet. She shared that she was also attracted to me but was married, which was the end of that. We did have a fun scene

Jeff with *Brian Carleton* -The Demon   where the demon possesses her; she comes into my room and tries to seduce me until I realize what's

239

happening and drive the evil spirit out of her.

One of the other leads in the film was *George P. Saunders*, a handsome guy about my age and a great actor. I found out later that he was the author of over a dozen novels and a professional Ballet Dancer on Broadway. George was also a successful screenwriter, with over 30 screenplays that were either optioned or produced into motion pictures. These included *Hard Corps* with *Jean-Claude Van Damme*, *Altitude* with *Dolph Lundgren* (*Expendables*) and *Denise Richards*, and *Perfect Target* with *Robert Englund* (*Freddy Kreuger*). (I would work with *Robert Englund* years later on the sci-fi series *SLIDERS*.) George also wrote *Magic Man* with *Billy Zane* (*Titanic*). George would become good friends with *Sheldon Lettich*, who directed *Double Impact*.

George played the role of an investigative reporter who doesn't believe in ghosts or goblins and was there purely to prove that my character was not a genuine psychic but a charlatan and a fake. He changes his tune pretty quickly when he has continual visitations by a beautiful ghost played by actress *Red Montgomery*, with whom his character eventually falls in love. Red was a lovely, blonde actress who looked a lot like *Kim Basinger* an A-List movie star in films like *LA Confidential*. I think that's why the producers cast her, they thought that might help sell the movie.

Red's character was a lost soul trapped in the house. Her sadistic husband had murdered her in the eighteen hundreds, and her soul was trapped, unable to move on to the afterlife. Red seemed to be a good actress as well, very committed to her craft; the problem was that Red was a Method actress, and for those of you who don't know what that is, Method actors do certain things to immerse themselves physically into a particular role beyond what is genuinely required.

Method acting is a technique in which an actor aspires to complete emotional identification with a part, based on the system evolved by *Stanislavsky* and brought into prominence in the US in the 1930s. Method acting was developed in institutions such as the *Actors' Studio* in New York City, notably by *Elia Kazan* and *Lee Strasberg*, and was associated with such actors as *Marlon Brando* and *Dustin Hoffman*. A classic example of Method acting was Dustin Hoffman's performance in the movie *Marathon Man*, starring *Laurence Olivier*, who was known as the world's best actor at the time. Olivier played a nazi who mistakenly kidnapped Dustin Hoffman's character and tortured him for information. Hoffman escaped and literally ran for his life until he was recaptured. By this time, his character was sweaty, out of breath, and exhausted from running away. They were ready to shoot this climatic scene in the film, but Dustin Hoffman was nowhere to be found. No one knew where he was, and the director started to panic.

A few minutes later, Hoffman showed up on set and said, okay, let's shoot it. Dustin was all sweaty, out of breath, and exhausted just like it said in the script. Olivier said to Hoffman, "Where were you? What happened?" Hoffman said, "Oh, I ran around the block a few times so I would be sweaty, breathless, and exhausted for the scene." Olivier looked at him and said, "Why don't you just try acting?"

That's Method Acting, doing something physically to prepare for a scene instead of just acting and creating all those emotions. I don't believe in it personally. No one should have to resort to that mental and physical anguish in order to get a specific emotion for a role. It's called acting for a reason. If you're playing a killer, does that mean you have to kill someone in order to know how a killer thinks and feels? I don't think so.

It turned out that Red was a Method actress; on the day of her scene she was in her trailer, we heard her crying. We thought something was terribly wrong, so the producers knock on the door and say "Red, are you okay? We can hear you're upset. Is there something we can do to help?" She goes, "No, leave me alone, I'm preparing." Okay. So they left her alone. She continued to cry for hours to work herself into this emotional frenzy. So, we're finally ready to shoot her scene later that day. She came out of her trailer, and looked terrible. The cameras started rolling, and it was obvious by her performance that she was completely and utterly emotionally drained. There was nothing left in the gas tank. She couldn't reach the emotional level of performance that was required, which was very disappointing for everyone. This integral scene in the movie would have been great for her and George, but it was a dud because she was emotionally exhausted. I felt terrible for George as this was his most emotional scene in the entire film. Instead of just acting and getting into a mindset of this tortured spirit, she felt she had to cry for hours in order to give a realistic performance. It just didn't work. That's Method.

Here's a message to all actors out there: Method is not always the best way to go. I always tell everyone to use the tools and training they need to do the job. Do whatever works best for you, but for me, Method isn't it. I come from a school that utilizes the *Meisner Technique*, which focuses on external sources for inspiration, with actors reacting to their fellow performers behavior and environment. Much of the Meisner technique is based around improvisation, enabling an actor to be spontaneous and respond to live moments (as in life) and rehearsed situations, which means being present in the scene. Learn the lines, forget the lines, and just put yourself in the situation, whether in a subway, in the middle of a flash flood, in a haunted house, or in outer space. Just be present in the scene, and whatever happens, happens. It's really reacting, not acting. The word acting is misplaced because if you're "acting" in a movie, you're not present; you're acting; it's false; it doesn't ring true, and it's not believable to the audience. So when I teach acting, I use the word reacting because it's all about listening; you're listening to the other person and responding to the words coming out of their mouths and the emotions they are exuding at that particular moment. It's grounded, and it's authentic. There's your first free acting lesson. See, my book just paid for itself. You're welcome!

Another day and we're filming inside the farmhouse and we're told from the get-go that it was haunted. The owner told us multiple stories of bizarre things that have happened that couldn't be explained except by supernatural forces. We're filming in the living room. It was interesting because we were doing a scene with this ancient chest that I found in the attic and I'm trying to summon the demon that inhabited the house. We were in the living room between takes, and I looked into the dining room. There was this beautiful antique chandelier hanging over the kitchen table, and right then, the lamp started to swing on its own, back and forth, back and forth, there was no earthquake no earthly disturbance. Because the chandelier was old and rusted, it squeaked as it swung back and forth; wee, wee, wee, wee, which caught the attention of everybody on the set. We were all staring at this lamp, swinging back and forth, in a pretty wide arc over the table, wee, wee, wee, wee, and were all just mesmerized watching this happen. Then, all of a sudden, it instantly stopped. We all looked at each other like, whoa, that was fucking weird, maybe this place was haunted, and the director said, okay, let's get back to work. So, we rolled the cameras and kept shooting.

It was very weird; a few other supernatural things happened during that shoot, which I can't remember at this time, it was many years ago, but it was super creepy, and it also reinforced what I've always believed, and that is that ghosts do exist, like aliens, there's too much information, there's too many sightings, there's too many instances for people to go, oh, yeah, that's not real. But it is; I can now speak from experience.

The Darkening was eventually bought by *Lionsgate*, which was, and still is, a major production company and distributor in Hollywood. *The Darkening* was renamed and released as *The Black Gate*. I would be privileged to work with Bill again on his next film as a director, a science-fiction/action-adventure called *Terminal Force* starring *Brigette Nielsen*.

Chapter 30

Terminal Force aka Galaxis

A few years after *The Darkening*, *Bill Mesa* contacted me saying he was going to be directing a Science Fiction/Action Adventure called *Terminal Force* starring *Sylvester Stallone's* ex-wife, actress *Brigitte Nielsen (Rocky IV, Red Sonja)*. Bill said he had already cast a Canadian actor by the name of *John H. Brennan (Badlands)* to be the male lead but wanted me to co-star in the film as one of the evil henchmen. *Terminal Force* told the story of a mythical gemstone created at the birth of the universe that could generate energy to sustain youth and vitality.

The tyrannical Kyla, played by *Richard Moll (Night Court)*, was desperately searching for the object to increase his villainous sphere of power. He successfully obtained the device after defeating its protectors on planet *Sintaria*. Meanwhile, Ladera (*Brigitte Nielsen*), a freedom fighter who had the power of invisibility, made her way to Earth to seek out a sister gem stone to stop Kyla. Once there, she meets Jed, played by Brennan, who accidentally acquired the gem. *Victor Menendez* (comedian *Fred Asparagus)* and his mercenaries also want the gem as compensation for a gambling debt owed by Jed, who banded together with Ladera to thwart Kyla's plans.

The story was a bit convoluted, but the action and visual effects more than made up for it.

Jeff with *Brigitte Nielson* as *Ladera*

It was a really fun role for me because I got to do all of my own stunts and got to shoot some pretty cool guns. There was one scene where we're in a big car chase after Brigitte. I'm leaning out the window of a Limousine with a semi-automatic assault rifle shooting at her at 80 miles an hour down the street. How many actors can say they did that? Brigitte ends up killing me towards the end of the movie. I'm hunting her down at an electrical power plant with my Street Sweeper (a massive gun that can shoot eight explosive rounds of ammunition and decimate whatever it shoots at). I manage to blow up everything in sight except for Ladera. She caught me by surprise and slammed my head into a steam pipe which exploded, burning my face off.

Jeff gives Brigitte a leg up on set

I remember the day we shot the limousine scene; it was about 103 degrees in the *San Fernando Valley*. Production had rented a limousine for the shoot that day, and in between takes, Brigitte would also have a cool, air-conditioned place to relax. She invited me inside the Limo with her to stay cool. We had a lot of scenes together, and really hit it off. She had a great sense of humor, and we laughed a lot. So I'm sitting next to her in the Limo and she puts her arm around me. As we talked I could smell vodka on her breath. A lot of actors are known to drink during the day during a shoot (and other things as well). The studios usually didn't care who did what, as long as you showed up on time, knew your lines, did a great job, and didn't cause any problems for production.

So Brigette and I were sitting in the limousine, and I got the feeling she was coming onto me. She asked, "Oh, do you know a fun club to go to in Hollywood tonight?" I was a little nervous and not quite sure what to say. Was she hinting about going out tonight? I always thought that she was very beautiful, super sexy, and a very

246

good actress.

Before she was as an actress, she was a supermodel because of her height of six feet, one inch and her incredible physique. Normally, I would gone along with her advances in the limousine. The problem was that her husband (at the time) was sitting right across from us. I'm super embarrassed and didn't quite know what to do because she has her arm around my shoulder, so I kind of just went with it. I kept looking at him and smiling like I was in a tough spot here; he didn't say anything; he just sat there. We kept talking until they needed us to start filming again. We got out of the Limo, and that was it.

It was a real rush for me and pumped me up to think that a beautiful international model and actress like Brigitte was interested

in me since I was still working my way up the ladder. We wrapped the film, and I never saw her again, but I have fond memories of working with her and everyone else on the film. I've written a very funny role for Brigitte in my ski and snowboarding comedy, *Snow Bunnies*. All I need is the millions of dollars to make it.

Spiderman **director** *Sam Raimi* **plays an interplanetary soldier**

An interesting bit of trivia; since the director, *Bill Mesa* had a long standing friendship and collaborative relationship with *Sam Raimi*, Bill offered him the opportunity to play a cameo role as a futuristic soldier that gets killed on the planets surface during an uprising.

Bill and I remain good friends to this day and look forward to working on oher genre projects together. Thanks again Bill for your confidence, friendship, and support.

Final Thoughts

Writing *I Was A Playboy Rabbit and Other Stories - A B-Movie Memoir* is the culmination of five years of hard work and determination. I must have rewritten it dozens of times adding and subtracting various parts of my life, to focus on the stories that I hope you have enjoyed and resonated the most.

Life is a series of experiences, good and bad which make us who we are as individuals. Sharing mine with you has been a way for me to give something back, to recognize the people that have inspired me, made an impact on me and have championed me along the way. Remember, what's most important is not our final destination, but life's journey that we need to appreciate.

In closing I'd like to share with you one of my favorite affirmations.

"You have been through a thousand things in your life that people don't even know about. You've experienced things that have shook you, changed you, broke you, built you and taught you that you are stronger than you ever thought possible. You are who you are because of all these things. So, the next time someone judges you based on a small part of what they see or what they think, remember who you are, remember how far you've come and keep moving forward because you don't have anything to prove to anyone but yourself."

I have been incredibly fortunate in my life in many ways, but most of all by having grown up in a supportive family and knowing the friends and lovers, both constant and fleeting, that I still cherish and will forever be part of me.

Thank you again for your love and support. May your future be bright, memorable, and full of joy. -Jeff Rector

Stay tuned for more stories and adventures in my next installment, "I Was A Playboy Rabbit and Other Stories: A B-Movie Memoir Volume 2"

www.ingramcontent.com/pod-product-compliance
Lightning Source LLC
Chambersburg PA
CBHW060924120626
46557CB00003B/863